Praise for *Police Pranks*

I have known Buzz for over 30 years. When I set out to take the account of the Long Beach Police Academy Association, he was actually the first director I was told to talk to. If I could win him over, others would follow. Thirty-one years later I am still working that account and the guys there have truly become a family in so many ways. Buzz has always been the one that was well respected, well spoken and solid on judgment. It is so nice that he memorialized so many stories from the past.

Police Pranks led me down memory lane, trying to resurrect the events and place the names with the faces of cops I happened to know over the years. I was able to guess so many of the individuals and could see the events taking place just as Buz described them in the book. I loved the short nature of the stories, moving from event to event with thc antics and languagc of a truc cop—no strings held back. Written by a good cop and perhaps even better storyteller and prankster, this book shows the day to day work of a big city cop in a light not usually, if ever, depicted in police books. Devoid of violence but loaded with the behind the scenes antics and stories about how cops to survive in the world they must work. From the stuttering "John" to the Chatty Kathy story, one cannot help but laugh at the situations they create and put themselves in. A great quick read for seeing the other side of the guys in blue.

—James E. Trott, Attorney, Huntington Beach, California

I have known Buz Williams for nearly 40 years. I have worked with him as a fellow officer and supervisor; I worked alongside him for years when we were both members of the Long Beach Police Officers Association Board of Directors; and I was his commanding officer in Juvenile.

I know Buz well. He is articulate, witty, a fabulous public speaker and a deep thinker. Buz's irreverence, his over-inflated sense of self-worth as a raconteur, and his seemingly unlimited supply of stories, practical jokes and recall of long forgotten minor misdeeds by others is legendary. Along with countless others, I have also been the object of his misplaced, so-called humor on many occasions. In fact, one of his stories in this book—a complete and utter misrepresentation of the facts—is about him targeting me.

Buz has a unique sense of humor and many of the stories he relates are true. That he has managed to remember these incidents so well—in many cases decades after they occurred—is symptomatic of his wretched wittiness. His long experience working in Vice—where investigators focus is on "victimless" and often, minor, unusual and bizarre crimes—provided someone with an already flourishing collection of material a gift of riches almost beyond comprehension.

On the other hand, if you are looking for a sophisticated, modern and mature sense of humor—well, don't bother to read this book. As a retired police chief, some of Buz's stories make me cringe. Cop humor, especially from the far distant past, is irreverent, unforgiving, childish and likely fits every 21st century "ism" that exists and perhaps more. That being said, cop humor is often the only wall between sanity and a very dark and dismal place.

The nature of police work and its toll on the soul is well documented. In today's world, humor is often not appreciated—even less so from the police. Police officers frequently feel they are expected to suppress their humor and be task perfect, dispassionate machines. Obviously, reality is different and Buz has always been one to poke, prod and expose the emotional, if occasionally inappropriate, side of our profession.

The best advice I can offer to you if you want to read this book and come away with why Buz's stories are so important, particularly in an age of epidemic police suicide, is to understand this quote about laughter from a character in sci-fi writer Robert Heinlein's novel, "Stranger in a Strange Land." Valentine Smith, a human born and raised on an emotionless Mars, says after spending time on earth, "I've found out why people laugh. They laugh because it hurts so much… because it's the only thing that'll make it stop hurting." In Police Pranks, Buz offers therapy—and that is never a bad thing.

—Timothy J. Jackman, Chief of Police (Ret)

Retired Sergeant "Buz" Williams has provided some gifted insights into the humor behind the badge in his book Police Pranks, Jokes, and Other Stories You Should Not Tell Your Children, the most aptly named title for a book that is sure to cause outward laughter, providing you have the requisite maturity to handle it. Sit back in your easy chair, put your feet up on the ottoman, and enjoy a couple hours of leisure reading as you laugh, guffaw, and try to suppress the giggles, chuckles and bursts of laughter that surely will follow in the book

—Retired LBPD Sgt. John J. Garry and current Mayor for Yerington, Nevada

Police Pranks, Jokes, and Other Stories Not Suitable for Children

Buz Williams

Genius Book Publishing

Los Angeles, California

Published by:
Genius Book Publishing
31858 Castaic Road, #154
Castaic, CA 91384
GeniusBookPublishing.com

ISBN: 978-1-947521-30-8

200420 Case

Table of Contents

About the Author

Richard F. "Buz" Williams, AKA "Edward One," was born at the Queen of Angels Hospital in Los Angeles, California in 1950. He grew up in the Westchester area of Los Angeles. At the age of four, Buz contracted primary tuberculosis and spent a year at the Olive View Sanatorium in Sylmar, CA. He went to twelve years of Catholic School: St. Jerome Elementary School and St. Bernard High School. He graduated from California State University at Long Beach in 1973, with a Bachelor of Science degree in Criminology. Buz spent six years in the California Army National Guard, from 1970 to 1976.

Buz grew up in a police family. His father, both his grandfathers, a great uncle, and a cousin all retired from the Los Angeles Police Department. He also had an uncle who retired from the Hawthorne (California) Police

Department. Buz worked 29 years on the Long Beach (California) Police Department (from January 1974 until December 2002) as a patrol officer, detective, sergeant, and detective sergeant. He worked as a sergeant in Booking, Vice Investigations, Auto Theft, Gang Detectives, Gang Enforcement and Juvenile. He served on the Long Beach Police Officers Association as Director, Secretary, Vice President and Editor of their magazine, *The Rap Sheet.*

Buz has been married to his wife, Judi, for 45 happy years. They have two grown, married sons, and three grandsons and one granddaughter. He and Judi moved to Prescott, Arizona in 2004. Buz wrote an opinion column for the Prescott Daily Courier from 2012 until 2017. He currently writes an online column for the Prescott eNews.

Disclaimer

While I am sure the vast majority of men and women in law enforcement, and their families, would not have a problem being mentioned on these pages, and might even consider it an honor, because we live in such litigious times, I have decided, in most instances, to use only first names.

Many will recognize the circumstances that led to the perpetration of their prank, or of their victimization, but proving "who done it" would be difficult, if not impossible, in a court of law. In addition, the world of law enforcement is not one for the overly genteel. The language and situations used herein reflect the humor that develops when in constant contact with crooks, ne'er do wells, muggers, murderers, thieves, perverts, hookers, peeping toms, and others who inhabit the nether regions of today's communities. Gallows, sick, or off-color humor often results from the constant interaction with these individuals, and the gut wrenching, often heartbreaking situations they cause or often find themselves in.

In addition, these stories in no way reflect on the dedication, courage, or professionalism of those in law enforcement. While many times those who work the streets in uniform are going from one call to another, there are often long periods of idleness due to weather or other reasons. While an idle mind may be the devil's workshop, a quiet radio also leads police to creative thoughts that in many cases lead to the pranks and jokes retold here.

Preface

By the beginning of my career at the Long Beach Police Academy on January 7, 1974, I had already heard dozens of stories about practical jokes that cops played on each other or on crooks. My father, both my grandfathers, a great uncle, and a cousin had all worked on the Los Angeles Police Department. My Uncle Don had been a sergeant on the Hawthorne, CA, Police Department. I had originally wanted to be a bank robber, but I didn't think I could survive a family reunion. In addition to the stories I'd already heard from my family, I heard more police tales when as a teenager I started going with my dad and his LAPD buddies on their annual fishing trips to the High Sierras.

Several of these narrations have been told to friends over the years. After the laughter dies down, someone will invariably make the comment, "Did you guys ever do any real police work?" The answer, of course, is "yes." Police officers, like everyone else, prefer to dwell on happier times. My grandmother told me that the only time she saw my grandfather, Lawrence E. "Benny" Williams, cry was when his partner, Vern A. Brindley, was killed in the line of duty. Grandpa was shot in the knee during the same incident that killed his partner. My dad never mentioned this incident to me, so I can only assume that my grandfather didn't dwell on that tragedy.

I did hear that my grandpa guffawed loudly when my grandmother confronted him with his hat, which had several condoms stuck in the hatband. His fellow vice officers had placed them there as a practical joke. Grandpa had apparently put his hat on without closely inspecting it and, when he got home, put it on the hat rack where my Grandma found it.

On my maternal side of the family, my Grandpa Harry Ellsworth Miller was also on LAPD. Once when he invited several coworkers and their spouses over to his house for a barbeque, one of the female guests, whom my Grandpa found a little too snooty, became the brunt of one of his jokes. When she approached him while he was chopping some vegetables, Grandpa Miller put a very sad look on his face. She asked him what was wrong. He immediately pulled his half-open pants zipper the rest of the way down, pulled out a turkey neck he had secreted there, and laid it on the cutting board saying, "This damn thing is always getting me in trouble." He then chopped it in half with a meat cleaver, accompanied by the panicked screams of the woman. These stories came from my own family, but they illustrate the type of humor, admittedly sometimes perverse, in which police officers engage, to relieve some of the stresses the job can cause.

Part 1: From Back in the Day

1: The Suitcase Surprise

A year or so after the end of World War II, some passengers waiting for buses or taxis at Union Station near downtown Los Angeles had their suitcases stolen from the curb. If the victim, often recently a released soldier or sailor with separation pay in their luggage, was temporarily distracted or had fallen asleep on the bus bench, a vehicle, usually containing two, but often three or four suspects, would drive up and snatch the suitcase and drive off. Stakeouts and other usual methods were unsuccessful in capturing the thieves.

Con Keeler, one of the detectives of the newly formed "Gangster Squad," had connections with the California State Department of Fish and Game. One of the Fish and Game officers had trapped a live bobcat in a farming area outside the city. Keeler obtained this bobcat and gingerly placed it in a suitcase. A block away, Keeler and some of the other Squad members were watching through binoculars. One of the detectives staggered up to the bus bench and placed the booby trapped, or rather bobcat trapped suitcase next to the bench. He sat down and, after a few minutes, let his chin drop to his chest feigning sleep.

Within ten minutes, a four-door sedan containing four male subjects pulled just past the bus stop. With the motor running, the man in the right rear seat got out of the car, grabbed the suitcase, and threw it in the backseat, following it in. The car took off at a high rate of speed. Half a block later the sedan went into a four-wheel skid. All four doors opened and all four suspects went sprinting in four different directions. Con told me that the bobcat jumped out of the car and walked slowly down the street. The car was impounded as an abandoned vehicle. No arrests were made in this case, but the suitcase snatches at Union Station never reoccurred.

2: The General Jorgensen Caper

My father, Richard F. "Dick" Williams, transferred from Patrol to the Gangster Squad in 1947, spending the rest of his career there. Somewhere around 1949, the Gangster Squad's name changed to the "Intelligence Division." In 1957, my dad and his partner, Bill Roberts, were in a near fatal accident. My dad went through the windshield of their unmarked police car and 172 stitches were required to sew up all the cuts on his face. Bill, who was driving, only needed 3 stitches on his face. Bill told everyone who visited them during their months' long recovery at the Central Receiving Hospital that, between him and my dad, they had 175 stitches in their faces.

Because of their work against organized crime, visitors were screened. While they were in the hospital, Dad and Bill had numerous visitors. The strangest guest they had was an eccentric individual with the moniker of General Jorgensen. The "General" frequented a bar that was a hangout for mobsters. My dad and Bill also could be found there in the course of their duties.

When the mobsters found out that Williams and Roberts were in the hospital, they came up with a plan to have General Jorgensen go see them. Jorgensen wore a uniform and almost always carried a trumpet that he would play on request. One of the crooks either placed an artificial turd or actually crapped in the General's trumpet. When he found the offensive matter in his trumpet, Jorgensen was livid and asked everyone if they knew who shit in his trumpet. When the mobsters were asked, they told the General that Williams and Roberts had been working on the defiled trumpet investigation when they crashed. The crooks directed Jorgensen to the hospital.

While lying in their hospital beds, a nurse came in and told Williams and Roberts that there was a General Jorgensen wanting to see them. She told the two detectives that he looked a little odd and she would send him on his way. They both thought that Jorgensen might raise their spirits a little after a week or so of the hospital boredom, so they told the nurse to send the General in.

Jorgensen marched into the room and demanded to know who had "shit in my trumpet?" When Williams and Roberts started to laugh, the General became upset and told them that this was no laughing matter. He had been told that Williams and Roberts knew who the perpetrator of this heinous crime was, and he demanded to know his identity. Since both of the detectives had suffered rib injuries and laughing caused them pain, they attempted to stifle, unsuccessfully, their belly laughs. The more incensed Jorgensen became, the more they laughed and winced in pain. Finally the nurse came in and sent the General on his way.

3: What Does That Make You?

My father was a certified tough guy. He was a ranger in the Pacific during WWII and made several rubber boat landings behind Japanese lines. He was taught how to kill with his bare hands. He was six feet three inches tall and weighed about 200 pounds. He had his nose broken at least a dozen times, the first when he was about three years old. After the 1957 car wreck, his face had scars that faded over time. He had a presence. That being the case, the only people he ever tried to intimidate were the organized crime hoodlums he came across in LAPD's Gangster Squad.

Although he wasn't intentionally menacing, few people would purposely antagonize him. There was one instance to which I was a witness when I was eight or nine years old. One hot summer day, my dad said that he was going to the liquor store and asked if I wanted to go with him. Since the Lisko brothers, who lived two houses down from us, weren't around to play with, I went with my dad to the liquor store. He parked his unmarked police car, a gray 1957 Ford Fairlane, next to another car in the parking lot of Stewart's Bottle Bar. There were three young guys in their late teens or early twenties wearing white tank tops (commonly called "wife beater" shirts) standing next to their car.

When my dad got out of the Ford, his door may have slightly bumped the other car.

As my dad and I were starting to walk toward the store, one of the young men called out, "Hey, man, your door hit my car."

Dad stopped, looked at the car, and said, "Sorry. It doesn't look like there is any damage," and started back toward the liquor store.

The young would-be tough guy then replied with, "Sorry, doesn't cut it, man. Fuck you."

My dad turned around, took two steps back, got right in the hood's face and said, "If there is going to be a fucking around here, I plan to be on the dick end of it. And if you follow that to its logical conclusion, that would make you a big pussy, wouldn't it?" and then he pushed the guy in the chest. "Is there anything else?" my dad queried.

The mouthy dude looked at his buddies, who were looking in other directions. After ten or twelve seconds of silence, my old man added, "I didn't think so." That was the end of it. I knew my dad could be a mean hombre, but I hadn't realized he was so damn witty, too!

4: Telephone Surprise

In the late 1940s and early 1950s, mobsters were trying, with some success, to take over the card clubs in Gardena, California. Organized crooks from the East were gaining a foothold in Southern California. While these clubs were not within the city of Los Angeles, the Intelligence Unit worked in them to get information on gangsters and their activities, and to minimize their traction in the state.

One day, my father went into one of the clubs. He wanted to see if the owner, who was being extorted by a mobster for a piece of his business, was in. My dad went to the bank of phones near the offices of the club and dialed the main number. From his phone booth, my dad could see into the glass-enclosed office. He saw the mobster in question answer the ringing phone. He had his back turned to the phone bank and away from the office door.

Dad asked, "May I speak to Bo?"

The mobster answered, "Who is this?"

My dad declared, "Tell him, this is Dick."

The bad guy said, "Are you that big, ugly L.A. Cop? If you were here, I would kick the shit out of you...."

While he continued to talk into the phone, my father let his handset gently drop from his hand, walked over to the office, opened the door, grabbed the mobster by the neck of his shirt and his belt, walked him out the front door of the club, kicked him in the ass, turned him around, and said, "Well, here I am. Why don't you try to kick the shit out of me now?"

The surprised crook did not attempt to engage my father in a street fight. He was shaking badly and just kept saying, "Man, that was cold. I didn't know you were here."

After telling me this story, my dad explained to me that a lot of people say things on the phone that they wouldn't have the balls to say to your face. He also said that this was the most satisfying phone call he had ever made.

5: Duck Hunting in Downtown Long Beach

Some legends grow out of practical jokes. Whether the following story is true or not is up for question, although two different training officers related this tale with very few differences. From World War II until the 1980s, Long Beach, California had a major United States Navy Base. As a result, the Long Beach Pike and the bars in the downtown area catered to sailors. When the fleet was in, sailors, both in uniform and in civilian clothes, populated these areas of Long Beach.

As the story goes, two graveyard shift patrolmen developed an idea to fool inebriated sailors into thinking that Long Beach Police officers were hunters of mythical skills. They gathered the proper equipment they would need and waited for the right climatological conditions. One foggy night, those conditions were perfect. The pranksters drove to the duck pond at El Dorado Park and shot a couple of ducks. Just before the bars closed at 2 AM, one of the cops walked up to the roof of a three story building next to one of the sailor bars on Long Beach Boulevard. With him, he carried a bag that contained the two dead ducks and a duck call.

The other officer stationed himself at the curb, ten or twelve feet from the front door of the sailor bar. He was holding his police shotgun at port arms, loaded with blanks, and was looking up into the fog. As the sailors started dribbling out of the bar they were attracted like a magnet to the stoic policeman, gazing up into the mist. After a group of four or five sailors had gathered, one finally asked the question the cops had been waiting for: "What are you doing?"

In a voice loud enough for his partner to hear three floors up, the patrolman on the street said, "I'm duck hunting. What's it look like?"

One of the swaying sailors asked the question that begged answering, "How are you gonna shoot ducks you can't even see?"

Again in his loud voice, the shotgun cop answered, "You don't have to see 'em, all you have to do is hear 'em." About that time, the upstairs policeman blew a few times on the duck call. The street cop then aimed the shotgun up into the fog and fired, ejected the spent round and jacked another round into the shotgun and fired again. Meanwhile, his partner on the roof threw one duck over the side, followed in rapid succession by the second duck.

The ducks landed near the officer and the astounded sailors. The policeman walked over, grabbed the two ducks, and walked past the awestruck sailors to his patrol car. He put the ducks in the backseat and then drove around to the alley to pick up his partner.

One wonders what those sailors told their shipmates, let alone their families when they returned home.

Part 2: Police Academy Follies

1: Recruits in Awe of a Veteran Police Officer

When I was in college at California State University, Long Beach, in 1969, I was hired for a position as a student worker for LAPD. One of the requirements for this job was a full LAPD physical. I had worked for three months in the Detective Bureau at Venice Division when I was notified that I had flunked the physical because I had a curvature of the spine. My appeal was denied. I was upset because of my family history at LAPD. In the summer of 1973, after I graduated from college, a friend of mine told me that the Long Beach Police Department was giving an entrance test. There were around 1500 applicants. I went with my buddy, took the written test, and was later given an oral exam. I finished at number 38 or 39.

On January 7, 1974, I reported for the first day at the Long Beach Police Academy. We recruits were too much in awe of what was awaiting us to even think about any pranks. Most of us didn't know anyone else in the class, or at least didn't know them very well. There were 22 men and 3 women. One thing happened that mesmerized all of us.

The Lieutenant, Doug, who was in charge of the Academy, came into our classroom to welcome us. Back in 1974, most cops smoked. There were no restrictions on where a person could smoke and there were butt cans in the classroom indicating that it was permissible there. In the middle of his speech, the Lieutenant pulled the last cigarette from his pack. He lit the cancer stick, crushed the pack, and nonchalantly tossed it backhand toward the nearest butt can, which was about 20 feet away. Twenty-five sets of eyes watched as the empty pack arced across the space and landed perfectly in the can. Without missing a beat, the Lieutenant gave a brief smile and continued with his oration as if he performed supernatural acts like this every day. Every recruit in the class was hoping that if they got nothing else out of the academy, they might learn how to act that cool while performing inexplicable deeds.

2: The Unknown Streaker

Every day, when we assembled before marching into class, we had an inspection. One morning about halfway through our 16-week academy, the Academy Sergeant announced that we would not have the inspection the next morning, but at the assembly after lunch instead. This unprecedented arrangement was the lead-in to two pranks. I was the victim of the first and the whole recruit class was the target of the second.

My classmate Don and I were having a prank war. I don't remember what I did to Don, but he more than got even. While we were waiting for our PT (Physical Training) officers to give us our inspection, Don pretended to inspect some of us. When he stood in front of me, Don stated, "This tie is too long." He then produced some scissors and cut off the last 10 inches off my tie. There was only five minutes before the 1 PM inspection and I was starting to panic. Fortunately, Don was prepared and gave me his extra tie seconds before the inspection began.

We were still waiting for the PT instructors to arrive when our Platoon Guide was ordered to call us to attention. We were at attention for a couple of minutes when suddenly we were streaked by a man wearing nothing but running shoes, a jock strap and a paper bag with eye holes cut into it. A popular game show at the time was *The Gong Show*, which featured a character who called himself "The Unknown Comic" and wore that same type of paper bag over his head. We recruits were pretty sure that the "Unknown Streaker" was one of our PT instructors, Arnie. He was already a legend on our department and this incident added to his reputation.

3: The Vicious Lie Prank

Don wreaked his revenge on me another time later in the academy. I was the proud owner of a fire engine red 1968 Ford Fairlane 500 Fastback. This was the car I drove to the academy every day. I lived in a large house in Manhattan Beach that I rented with four other guys. I drove about 15 miles of Southern California freeways to Long Beach, picked up my classmate Brad, and continued on to the Academy. The only variation was when it was Brad's or my turn to buy two dozen donuts for our class and the Academy staff. (Yes, even though we were just recruit cops, we already loved our donuts.) I reversed the same course on the way home.

One day after lunch, I was fortunate to get a parking space in the front row in the area where we recruits parked. I was able to back into the spot which meant that

Brad and I would be able to make a quick getaway at the end of the day. The last period of the day had the class separated into four or five small groups. Unfortunately for me, my group was the last to finish and when Brad and I reached my car, several of our classmates were already standing in the parking lot talking. As we were driving out of the parking lot, several of them started waving and saying things like, "Bye, Bye, Buz," "Drive safely," and other such inane phrases. This was so out of the ordinary that I turned to Brad and asked, "What's up with them?" Brad just shrugged. I dropped him off a few minutes later. I then drove onto the on-ramp and entered the sea of cars on the northbound San Diego Freeway. In the stop-and-go traffic, many cars passed me at various times on both my right and left. The people in those vehicles would turn, look at me, and smile. I thought to myself, "Boy, people on the road are friendly today!"

I drove to what was essentially our "frat house" in Manhattan Beach, doffed my khaki recruit uniform, showered and shaved, put on a shirt and jeans, and drove to my fiancé's house in Torrance. While having dinner with my future wife, Judi, and her wonderful mother, Dorothy, there was a knock on the door. When my betrothed answered the door, it was the little boy who lived next door. "Judi, what's written on the back of your boyfriend's car?"

Judi told him she didn't know and why didn't we all go and look. This we did. Much to my embarrassment, written in white shoe polish against the fire engine red background, in capital letters, was the phrase, "I WEAR THE WORLD'S SMALLEST JOCK STRAP." (It was, by the way, a VICIOUS LIE.) I was quite lucky in that the writing came off easily with a damp cloth. Judi still decided to marry me despite this libelous slander. I was able to drive back to Manhattan Beach without suffering more toothy grins from other drivers.

The next day, through a diligent investigative process (classmates were lining up to rat out the mastermind), I found out that my old nemesis, Don, was behind the whole caper. I also found out that I had dodged a bullet. Originally, Don had written, "FUCK THE CHP" (California Highway Patrol), but some of the more mature classmates had talked him into changing it. Thinking back to 1974, if I had been spotted by the California Highway Patrol with that provocative statement on the back of my car while driving on one of their freeways, I might have been pulled over and give a gratuitous lesson in the proper use of the baton, wrist locks, shackles, and whatever other innovative ideas came into the Chippys' minds. Thank God they got Don to change it!

4: The Swiss Cheese Sweater

As I stated before, we had three women in our class. We all went through the same training, including the running, PT, and firearms training. Wednesday was our firearms training day. One of those Wednesday mornings had been a bit chilly, and Marsha had worn a sweater.

The pistol range only had a dozen or so lanes, so our 25 class members had to fire in shifts. The course, at that time, consisted of shooting from the 7 yard line, moving back to shoot from the 15 yard line, and then moving to the 25 yard line to shoot from there. At the 15 yard line there was a short barricade that the shooter knelt behind.

By the time we started the qualification training at the pistol range, the sun had come out from behind the clouds and it had warmed up considerably. As Marsha moved back to the 15 yard line, she took off her sweater and hung it on one side of the barricade. She left it there when she went back to the 25 yard line. When the recruits on either side of Marsha saw this, they nodded at each other. After shooting at the 25 yard line the shooters were instructed to retrieve their silhouette targets for scoring. After getting her target, Marsha stopped at the 15 yard line to retrieve her sweater. Immediately, she noticed there were several bullet holes in it. Some of our classmates claimed that Marsha inadvertently shot her own sweater. I personally believe that one or both of the recruits in the lanes next to Marsha couldn't resist shooting her sweater when they saw it hanging on the barricade.

5: The Sight of Blood

Toward the end of the Academy, after PT one day, we were instructed to drive to the Red Cross in Long Beach. Our instructors met us there and lined us up to give blood. After that, we were dismissed from there, since it was almost the end of our day anyway. I went directly to Judi's house because she and her mother had invited me over for spaghetti dinner. When I walked in, Judi noticed the white gauze bandage on my right arm. When she asked, I told her I had given blood an hour or so before.

Judi asked me why I hadn't taken off the bandage and I told her that the nurse told me to keep it on for four hours. Judi said she had given blood dozens of times and that you could take the gauze off after about half an hour. I thanked her for her opinion, but told her I would take the advice of a medical professional over hers. Mistake!

Partway through the meal, Judi pointed at my bandaged arm and said, "It looks like you sprung a leak." I looked down and saw that my previously white gauze bandage was now crimson. I started sucking in air and applying pressure to my arm. I looked up when I realized that Judi and her mom were laughing uncontrollably. When her mother had diverted my attention, Judi had poured a large spoonful of spaghetti sauce on my bandage. (Not being one to hold a grudge, I still married Judi a couple of months later.)

Part 3: Hitting the Bricks

1: Graffiti in Stall Three

After we graduated from the Academy, we entered a training period and were assigned to the Patrol Bureau. In Long Beach, we were fortunate to have a work schedule of ten hour days, four days a week. Our class was divided up among the three watches: Watch I was the graveyard shift. The hours were from 10:30 PM to 8:30 AM. Watch II had the daytime hours from 7:30 AM to 5:30 PM. Watch III went from 4:30 PM to 2:30 AM.

My first month out of the Academy, I was assigned to Watch I. I arrived at the station around 9 PM and got dressed. Until you've done it for a while, donning a police uniform is kind of a chore. The uniform itself isn't that bad, but after you put on the shirt, pants, belt and shoes, you then have to put on the "Sam Brown," the police gun belt. This usually consists of four "keepers," which are leather snaps that are placed under the pants belt and are snapped closed after the Sam Brown is in place. The Sam Brown holds a lot of equipment: gun and holster, spare ammo pouches, handcuff case or cases and, at that time, mace. It was heavy and took me some time to put on, which was why I went to the station early.

From the locker room, I walked to the Squad Room and saw nobody was there. I looked at my watch and discovered I was forty-five minutes early. I decided to make use of the men's room. I went into the third stall. I then had to unsnap the keepers, take off my gun belt, and loosen my other belt in order to drop my drawers. Having finally accomplished this unfamiliar task, I sat on the commode. While taking care of business, I started reading some of the graffiti that was written on the walls. "The Red Ant sucks the big one" meant nothing to me. "Sergeant So and So is an asshole." That one I had heard. Then I noticed something written near the bottom of the door to the stall. I had to lean way forward to see it. Squinting, I read, "You are now shitting at a 45 degree angle." I laughed out loud and then started looking around to see if there was a "candid camera" filming my reaction. Of course there wasn't, but I immediately realized I was going to like working with a bunch of guys who had this kind of sense of humor.

2: Pranks and Revenge: Dave versus Jim

Jim and Dave had been pulling practical jokes on each other since the Police Academy. After their field training was completed they were both assigned to Watch III. Dave was able to get the combination to Jim's locker and moved the buckle on Jim's Sam Brown belt forward a notch, making the belt longer. (The Sam Brown has a buckle that can be moved forward or backward to accommodate those with larger or smaller waists.)

Jim, who was constantly fighting the "battle of the bulge," would hold his belt out and say to all the other cops getting dressed, "Look at how much weight I've lost since last week." The next week, Dave snuck into Jim's locker and moved the buckle back a notch or two. Jim changed into his uniform and then attempted to put on his Sam Brown. Jim didn't say a word as he tried to hook the belt together. Everyone but Jim knew what was happening and had a good laugh watching Jim unsuccessfully trying to buckle his belt.

The ultimate "belt gotcha" came when Jim's partner, Rich, who had a 28 inch waist, gave Dave his old Sam Brown. Although the buckles are adjustable, the belts themselves come in different sizes. A belt that fit Rich could have the buckle adjusted to fit a waist from 26 to 30 inches. Dave went into Jim's locker, took Jim's holster, handcuff case, ammo pouches, baton holder ring and key ring off Jim's Sam Brown. He then put them on Rich's old one and hung it in Jim's locker. When Jim related the story later, he said that after trying to put the Sam Brown around his waist, he realized that he would be lucky if it might fit around his calf!

That wasn't the only thing Dave did when he burgled Jim's locker. One time, he cut the third button from the top off all of Jim's uniform shirts. We were having an inspection on this particular day, so Jim put on one of his shirts and noticed that the third button was missing. He put that shirt back in his locker and tried on the next one, only to find that shirt was also missing the third button. Jim found that all of his shirts were missing the same button. He began to suspect that perhaps someone was getting into his locker and took steps to find the culprit.

Prior to Jim discovering who the offender was, Dave struck one last time. He purloined Jim's uniform pants, took them to the cleaners, and had the hem on one leg sewn up 4 inches higher than the other. Still unaware that he faced more treachery in the locker room than on the streets, Jim came to work, put on his uniform, and walked into the Squad Room. As he was looking for a seat, one of the other officers asked in his felony voice, "Hey, Jim, who's your tailor?" Of course, every cop in the room looked and saw the mismatched pants legs. As titters and guffaws filled the Squad Room, Jim looked down at his pants and realized he'd been had. Again!

3: Jim's Revenge is a Twofer

When Jim finally found out that his nemesis was Dave, he began plotting his revenge. He noticed that Dave always placed his uniform shoes on top of his locker after they were shined. One day, when Dave had gone home at the end of watch, finding Dave's shoes in their usual place, Jim took the shoes from atop the locker and placed the contents of two jars of Vaseline inside each shoe. The next day, Dave found a squishy surprise when putting on his uniform shoes.

Six months later, Jim and his family went to another of our classmates' homes for a barbecue. He was relating the story of his revenge to his host, Bruce. Jim was a little surprised that Bruce wasn't laughing, but since Bruce is not the demonstrative type, Jim continued with his story. When Jim arrived at the part of the story where he had pushed the Vaseline to the toes of Dave's shoes, Bruce stopped him and said, "And then you wiped your greasy hands all over a towel that was hanging on the locker next to Dave's, didn't you?" Jim responded, "Yeah, how did you know?" Showing emotion for the first time, Bruce added in a loud voice, "Because that was my towel and when I started drying off after I took a shower that day, I got Vaseline all over myself!"

4: How I Learned to Hate Motor Officers

Motor officers are a different breed of cop. In most departments, even their uniforms are different. They wear helmets and knee high motor boots. This makes them feel like they are elite. They also get more pay because it is considered "hazardous duty." I agree it is more dangerous. Isn't dodging bullets, the occasional rock, bottle, and profanities dangerous enough without having to be on the lookout for wayward cars, SUVs, or minivans? Another difference is that regular patrol officers answer citizens' calls for service and want to stop crime and arrest criminals. Motor officers' main focus is to spot traffic violations and write tickets. I bet if someone took a survey of people who were issued what they thought were "chicken shit" tickets, 95% of them received those traffic tickets from motor officers. I have many friends who are or were motor officers. I think all of them are crazy for having tested fate by riding "suicycles," but when they aren't working, they are almost human. The following story illustrates why I developed a career-long animosity toward the elite motor squads.

My second week out of the Academy, my training officer, Gerry, let me drive for the first time. We were working the graveyard shift in North Long Beach. About midnight, as we were approaching a major intersection, Gerry asked, "Did you just see that car run the red light?" I had not seen it, but there was only one car that had crossed in front of us, so I knew which car he was referring to. "Pull it over and write the driver a ticket."

I pulled over the sedan and, just like I learned in the Academy, I stopped our squad car in the offset position, got out and started walking to the driver's side of the sedan. With my flashlight in my left hand and my holster unsnapped, I approached the trunk of the vehicle. I had already noted that there was a passenger in the front seat. I was looking in the backseat to see if there were any other passengers. Just as I reached the rear bumper, there was a very loud pop, like a gunshot. I immediately jumped over the trunk of the car and looked to the left.

At that time on our police department, motor officers wore tan khaki uniforms. Patrol officers wore blue wool uniforms. One of our lowlife motor officers had made his motorcycle backfire as he passed right next to me. I saw this miscreant Harley jockey wobbling, barely staying on his bike because he was laughing so hard as he rode off into the distance. I turned and saw my training officer, Gerry, also laughing uncontrollably. The driver and passenger in the car were also laughing. The four or five people on the sidewalk were cackling, too. After leaping over the trunk, I found myself standing near Gerry. He whispered, "Sometimes discretion is the better part of valor. Why don't you just go tell the driver to watch the red lights." I did this and as I slowly and shamefully ambled back to the squad car, I swore I would get even with the fraternity of motor cops whenever I could.

5: My Revenge

In training, we rookies worked with training officers for three months, one month in each of the Watch shifts. After this three-month period, we were assigned to our permanent watch (which for rookies was always either Graveyard or Nights) and were scheduled to work with a senior officer until the detail sergeant thought we were trained sufficiently to choose our own partner.

A year or so later, I was working with Denny, who had been hired on Long Beach the same time I was, but had transferred over from the L.A. County Sheriffs. One afternoon, I was driving up to our beat in North Long Beach on the 710 Freeway in the slow moving, rush hour traffic. I looked in the rearview mirror and saw two motor cops on their bikes behind me. Long Beach Motor cops had recently changed to blue wool uniforms.

I decided that now was the perfect time to wreak my revenge on these "traffic officers." We were driving the standard police vehicle of the time, a mid '70s Dodge with a big V8 engine. We were traveling about 20 miles per hour. With the car in gear, I turned the ignition off and started coasting. 10 seconds, 20 seconds. At about 25 seconds, Denis gave me a side glance and said, "You're going to blow out the muffler."

"I don't give a shit," I answered. At 30 seconds, I turned the ignition back on and the Dodge exploded with a huge backfire.

The motor cop on the right swerved to the right and almost laid down his bike. It was obvious that the motor cop on the left was an old salt. He stood on his pegs, leaned over his windshield, and gave us the okay sign. At the next exit, which I believe was Pacific Coast Highway, the two motor officers went around us and down the off-ramp. It was only then that we saw that they were Los Angeles Police motor officers, not Long Beach. I didn't feel bad. All motor officers are evil when on duty!

6: In the Interest of Justice

I was working with John, a senior officer. We were going southbound on Alamitos approaching Broadway. Broadway is a one-way street going eastbound until it reaches that intersection. The four eastbound Broadway lanes separate at Alamitos. The two lanes on the north side of Broadway have to turn left onto northbound Alamitos after the traffic-lighted intersection. The two south lanes can continue eastbound. There is, or was, a triangular shaped island at the intersection on Broadway that separated the four lanes.

This occasionally caused some confusion for those traveling southbound on Alamitos approaching Broadway. It looks as if there are two intersections there. On this particular night, the car in front of our squad car came up parallel to the triangular-shaped island, momentarily hit the brakes and then sped through the light that had just turned red. I activated my red flashing lights, carefully drove through the intersection and pulled the offender over to the right curb. After getting out of the squad car, I walked up on the driver's side of the car while John watched the passenger side.

There was no passenger, only the driver. This was near an area of the city that had a large gay population. I don't know if the driver was gay, but he was very effeminate. He excitedly told me that he knew I had pulled him over because he had run a red light. He said that he was confused by the intersection. He was very cooperative. He handed me his driver's license and registration. As I was writing him the ticket, I told him that it was confusing at that intersection, but that I had to write him a ticket because all of the people on the street and in other cars saw him run the red light right in front of our squad car. I advised him that if he fought the ticket, the judge might understand his confusion and dismiss the case. As he signed the ticket, he profusely thanked me for my advice. John just looked at me and rolled his eyes.

A few weeks later, I received a subpoena to traffic court. One has to understand that motor officers go to traffic court almost daily because of all the traffic violations they write. A traffic sensitive patrol officer might write four or five tickets a week, whereas a motor officer may write twice that many in a day. So patrol officers don't go to court nearly as often, maybe a couple or three times a month. When a patrol officer goes to court, it is usually for a criminal case, such as a drunk driver, car thief, burglar or robber.

At that time, in the Long Beach Municipal Court, motor officers would sit in the jury box in the traffic court while they waited for their case to be called. On this particular day, my case was called first. I walked past the rail and the judge asked me what had happened. I looked at my copy of the ticket and told the judge about the car in front of us running the red light, southbound on Alamitos to eastbound on Broadway. The judge then turned to the defendant and asked him what had happened.

In the same excited, effeminate way he had spoken to me after running the red light, the driver told the judge, "Everything the officer said was exactly right. He was so nice and courteous. But I have to say that I was just so confused by that intersection. I thought that I was in the middle of it and so I just drove through. This officer told me that if I fought the ticket, the judge might understand my confusion and lessen the fine or dismiss it."

I glanced over at the jury box. The knee length, spit shined boots only exacerbated the condescending smirks on the faces of the motor officers. The judge then turned back to me and said, "I was at that same intersection yesterday and the same thing happened to me. It is very confusing there."

"Officer Williams, would you mind if I dismissed this case in the interest of justice?"

I told the judge, "No, your honor," and under my breath I whispered, "I just want to get the hell out of here." As I walked out of the courtroom, I again peeked at the jury box. Two of the motor officers winked at me and a third blew me a kiss. As I've stated before, motor officers are evil!

7: Dennis and Doc Bryant

About a year after graduating from the Police Academy, I started working with Dennis. Our hire dates were the same, and we were both in our early twenties. I was married but Dennis was single.

One night while we were on patrol, Dennis told me that he would have to go to his doctor, Dr. Bryant. Dr. Bryant was a very good doctor and had a thriving private family practice that he ran on Pacific Avenue in Long Beach. He was also one of our police surgeons who came into our jail and examined all the inmates.

I asked Dennis what particular ailment would cause him to seek treatment from a medical professional. He told me that he was experiencing a burning sensation when he urinated. "Sounds like gonorrhea to me, Denny," I said authoritatively. Dennis told me that he didn't think that was the case, implying, but not overtly saying that his love life was not that frisky at that particular time. In fact, Dennis had broken up with his girlfriend about six months earlier and unfortunately had been celibate since then.

The next week, I asked Dennis how his medical exam had turned out. His response was, "That damned Doc Bryant." I was taken aback and inquired how Dennis could say such a thing about such a well respected member of our local medical community.

Dennis then told me that he had gone to Doc Bryant's office and, after a brief exam, the good doctor had required Dennis to give him a urine sample and told him to come back in a couple of days. Denny told me that when he went back, he was sitting in the waiting room with several young women, some with their small children. Doc Bryant walked by the door between the waiting room and the examination rooms and saw Dennis. The good doctor stopped in the doorway and called out, "Hey, Dennis!"

He looked up and asked, "Yes, Doc?"

At that point, in a loud voice, Doc Bryant said, "You'll be happy to know you don't have the clap!" Dennis said a couple of the young mothers wrinkled their noses at him and moved with their children to the other side of the waiting room!

8: "I'm Ronald Reagan"

One night, Dennis and I were dispatched to a garage apartment in the central area of Long Beach to assist a woman who had been locked out of her apartment by her boyfriend. The young woman we met was a nurse at one of our local hospitals and had to go to work. She told us that her boyfriend "was acting crazy" and wouldn't let her in the apartment to get ready for work. We went up the stairs to her apartment and knocked on the door. After several knocks and us yelling, "Police!" there was no response.

After several attempts, the woman asked if she could borrow my big Kel-lite flashlight. I handed it to her and she took it and smashed out the window next to the door. She then proceeded to climb through the window and unlock the door. She let us in and we found that the boyfriend was not in the apartment. As Dennis and I were walking away from the apartment, the woman yelled down to us that her boyfriend was drunk and was staggering up the alley behind the apartment.

We watched as he fumbled through the gate from the alley and it was obvious that he was intoxicated on something, although he didn't smell of alcohol. We leaned him up against the fence and patted him down. His eyes were bulging and he was generally non-responsive. We decided to arrest him and take him to the Narcotics Division where they would determine what drugs this fool had ingested. (Later we came to recognize these symptoms as the results of PCP, also known as "angel dust.")

After we handcuffed him, he gratuitously blurted out, "I'm Ronald Reagan." At that time, Ronald Reagan was the Governor of California. This tall skinny black man was obviously not the still well known actor, governor, and future president.

At this point, our suspect went completely limp. It was almost as if the bones in his body had just disintegrated. He lost all coordination and couldn't walk. We started dragging his body to our police car. As we were doing this, two young men saw us and started toward us, one of them saying, "Hey, man, why do you have to drag him like a dog?" Their demeanor was hostile so I let Dennis continue to drag our suspect toward the car while I stopped and turned to prevent the two antagonists from trying to snatch our prisoner.

I told them, "If he would walk like a man, we wouldn't have to drag him like a dog." The two then held their ground while we put the suspect in the backseat of our black and white.

Dennis got into the backseat with the prisoner, and I got behind the steering wheel. I had only driven about half a block when the suspect's boot kicked me "right upside" my head. This caused me to swerve and almost strike a parked car.

The suspect started yelling, "I'm Ronald Reagan. I'm Ronald Reagan."

Dennis started yelling to me, "Give me your flashlight."

As I handed Dennis my Kel-lite, I told him, "Don't hit him in the head! Don't hit him in the head!" I continued driving and trying to dodge our prisoner's boot, which was still flying around in the proximity of my head. In those days, the Long Beach police cars did not have cages between the front seats and the backseats.

Of course, Dennis hit the suspect in the head several times and then put him in the carotid restraint hold. Dennis told me that it was okay, that the suspect's head wasn't bleeding. When Dennis released the restraint hold, however, blood started spurting like Mount Vesuvius. Dennis tells me that maybe we should take the suspect to St. Mary's Emergency Room. As I drove there, the suspect kept repeating that he was "Ronald Reagan." Dennis and I both knew that if the suspect said this at the hospital, the doctors and nurses would tell us that he would have to be transported to the psych ward at Harbor General Hospital and we would be out of service for a lot longer. We kept telling him that he had to keep his mouth shut and not say a word at the hospital.

Unfortunately, as we were bringing him into the ER, one of the docs stopped, looked at the suspect's head and asked, "What do we have here?"

Before we could stop him, the suspect yelled out, "I'm Ronald Reagan!"

At that point, the doctor looked at us and said, "He's a 5150 (which is the Health and Safety Code section for a mental patient). You'll have to take him to Harbor General."

The saga continued when we took the suspect to Harbor General. While we were waiting for a room to open up, we sat the suspect on the floor in the hallway. The suspect kept stating that he was Ronald Reagan and trying to kick anyone who walked by.

To prevent anyone from getting hurt by our suspect, Dennis stood on the suspect's feet. A nurse, who was giving a tour to a group, saw Dennis standing on our suspect's feet and told the group, "I don't why this cop is brutalizing this prisoner by stepping on his feet." Dennis stepped off the suspect's feet and "Ronald Reagan" proceeded to kick her in the leg. Dennis told her that was why he was standing on the "poor guy's" feet. In a huff, she turned and guided her group away. Dennis stepped back on the suspect's feet, preventing him from kicking any of the retreating group.

The nurse must have notified security, because an enormous black man in a security uniform arrived and asked us what was going on. When we told him, he nodded, knowingly. Finally a room was clear and we handcuffed the suspect to the gurney and stood in the doorway.

A few minutes later a doctor went into the room and, as we followed him in, he turned to us and said, "I don't want you officers in here." We went out of the room and the doctor closed the door behind us.

The security guard smiled, shook his head, and said, "I tell these doctors and I tell them, but they just don't listen."

A few short minutes later, the doctor came out wiping bloody spit off of his face. "I can't examine him right now, you've just got him too agitated," the doctor stated.

Dennis responded, "On the contrary, doctor, he was quite calm 'til you got here."

A few minutes later, the doctor returned and told us that four or five stabbing victims were coming in from a gang fight so we needed to take our prisoner to the jail ward at County General Hospital.

As we were wheeling our suspect out of Harbor General in a wheelchair, a group of firefighters, who were in paramedic training, stopped us and asked if we would let them bandage our suspect's head. We agreed and they proceeded to wrap our suspect from the top of his neck to the top of his head. There were no openings for his eyes and just a small opening for his nose to breathe. Once his eyes were covered, our suspect, who had been squirming, kicking, and fidgeting the whole time, became virtually inanimate. It was Dennis's turn to drive, so I got in the backseat with the suspect. The suspect was so motionless that three or four times during the drive up to County General, I checked his pulse, thinking he might have died!

Once at County General, we took him up to the 13th floor jail ward. We seated him on a gurney and, at the direction of the LASO Sergeant, removed his cuffs. Because he was so docile at that time, the sergeant didn't re-cuff the suspect. Dennis and I thought that the sergeant had probably just made rank because he looked so well groomed for the jail. His uniform was pristine and pressed with two creases in the front and three in the back. The sergeant then said, "Let's see what he looks like," and started to unravel the gauze bandage. This made the blood on the suspect's head start to ooze again. As soon as the bandage was off the suspect's eyes, they again bulged out.

After a couple of seconds, the suspect shook his head, and four or five lines of blood streaked across the front of the sergeant's previously immaculate uniform shirt. The sergeant looked down, saw the red stripes on his tan uniform, and gasped, "You fucking asshole." At that point five or six deputies appeared from out of nowhere and jumped on the suspect to restrain him. The sergeant looked over his shoulder at us and told us we could go. We happily left to drive back to Long Beach and file our reports.

Part 4: Juvenile Detectives

1: Doc Simonian and the Sensitive Gunshot Wound

After about two years in Patrol, the Department started pulling officers from our Academy class and reassigning us. With our low seniority, Dennis and I heeded the call to leave patrol before we were transferred to one of the "inside" assignments at the Booking Desk, Front Desk, the jail or Communications. We both transferred to the afternoon J-Car detail. J-Car was a plain clothes job that handled radio calls and other problems involving juveniles.

Another of our police surgeons was Dr. Simonian. He was a big barrel-chested guy with a loud deep voice, as I recall. One night as I was getting off the elevator about a quarter to four PM, I heard loud deep raucous laughter emanating from the juvenile holding cells. (At that time, we could still put the little darlings who were arrested for committing crimes into jail cells.)

We were looking toward the cell area, but couldn't see anything. The laughter died down after about a minute and then Doc Simonian could be heard asking one of the jailed juveniles, "Okay, kid, tell me again how you shot yourself in the dick." This young delinquent had decided to go out and commit a robbery with a stolen gun. As he put the gun in the front of his waistband, he accidentally pulled the trigger, shooting himself in a most sensitive area!

2: Mimicking the Dutchman

Working outside on the streets was always preferable to working in the office. When working the J-car, one wore a coat and tie, and drove a "heat short," a plain car that every thug in the world recognizes as a police car. Our main duty was to handle complaints and crimes regarding juveniles. If a call went out on the police radio regarding juvenile suspects, we would jump on it if we were near, or volunteer to take it over if it was in another part of Long Beach. One of the good things about working juvenile was that, by working in plain clothes and in a plain car we were able to go into areas where a black and white patrol car and uniform cops immediately stood out.

While working the afternoon J-Car, I partnered quite often with Fred. Fred and I have remained good friends, which is a credit to his sense of humor, considering the pranks I've pulled on him. Fred was born in Holland and did not immigrate to the United States until his mid-teens. As a result, Fred has a slight accent which I am able to mimic at will.

Working this shift required us to work "inside" about four days a month, answering phones and booking juvenile suspects. It didn't take me long to pick up on the way Fred answered the phone. "Juffenile, Fred, can I hep you?" One night when Fred and I were assigned inside, we were taking turns answering the phones. Fred was just hanging up, after telephonically assisting a citizen, when the other phone at the Juvenile front desk began to ring. I answered, "Juffenile, Fred, can I hep you?" I answered the caller's questions in my best Dutch accent and when the citizen was satisfied, I hung up the phone.

Fred jumped all over me, "Why are you toking like me on the phone?" I told Fred that I hated to talk to people on the phone because they said things on the phone they didn't have the balls to say in person. I told him that one of these days someone would say something on the phone that irritated me so much that I'd tell them to go screw themselves, or words to that effect. Fred jumped up and said, "Well, then they'll think it's me!"

I just smiled and said, "Now you understand."

3: The Dutchman Gets Even

For another couple months or so, I continued responding periodically to phone calls to the Juvenile Bureau with my Dutch accent, until the following happened. Fred and I were again working inside and it was my turn to answer the phone. When it rang, I picked it up and said, "Juffenile, Fred, can I hep you?"

The caller reacted by stating, "Oh, yes, Detective Fred, you were out at our house last week about the problem with my neighbor's kids." Since I had been on vacation the week before, I had not worked with Fred and hadn't the faintest idea about what the problem was.

I looked at the phone and said, "Oh, yah, sure, just a minute," and put the call on hold. "Fred," I said as I indicated the blinking light on the phone, "this one's for you."

With a wickedly spiteful smile, Fred declared, "Oh, no. You wont to toke like me, then toke like me." I had to spend the next twenty minutes finding out what the problem was the week before, what action Fred and his partner had taken, and answer the citizen's inquiries, all in my fake Dutch accent.

That cured me from impersonating Fred on the phone for the next couple of years!

4: Back at You, Fred

It didn't prevent me from messing with Fred, though. When we worked in the field, we had to call the Juvenile Bureau every hour or so, to see if they had any non-emergency juvenile problems that had been called in. To keep the radio free for more important communications, we would call in from a call box. One, night, when Fred was at the front desk answering phones and I was in the field working with another Juvenile detective, we decided to have some fun with Fred. We called in and Fred answered the phone in his usual manner. I responded in my best southern drawl, "Yeah, Mr. Fred, I bin lookin' fo my son and he caint be found. Is he there?"

"How du I know? You don tell me your son's name or a description so how can I tell?" Fred answered in a slightly angered tone.

"Well, I called his school and he haint there, so I checked the hospital and he haint there, neither. So now I'm checkin' with ya'll to see if he bin arrested. Has he?" I inquired.

In a louder, more irked voice, Fred asked, "How du I know if you are not telling me his name or what he looks like? What da heck is his name?"

I knew I had gotten to Fred so I gave him just one more little push, "I'm sorry, Mr. Fred. Don't ya'll get mad at me." Then I reverted back to my normal voice and added, "It's just me, Fred. Do you have anything for us?"

Now Fred was really galled. "You son of bitch, you make me so mad!" Then he hung up on me.

A week or so later, I was working inside. I answered a phone call and I heard the high pitched voice of a Dutchman attempting to sound like a Southerner asking, "Is my daughter there?"

It didn't take Dick Tracy to know that this was Fred, so I responded, "No, Fred, she's not here. Why do think she would be in Juvenile?"

For a few seconds, there was silence on the line and then Fred asked, "Damn, how did you know it was me?"

5: "Class"

Fred and I had to go to Juvenile Court one day on a juvenile we had arrested. As we were walking down the hallway, we passed Norm, one of the two detectives on our Department that worked gangs at that time. When Norm saw Fred, he smiled and said, "Hello, Class!" Fred laughed and responded with, "Hey, Class, good to see you." As Fred and I continued walking, my curiosity got the best of me and I queried, "Fred, what is this 'Class' thing all about?"

After we checked in with the Juvenile DA, Fred told me all about it. He and Norm were working together in a squad car. It was a warm summer night, but it was raining heavily. Norm was driving down an alley in a residential area when the headlights illuminated two naked bodies, a male atop a female. They were apparently involved in a sexual liaison right in the middle of the alley, in the rain, with the runoff swirling around them. Being seasoned officers, both Norm and Fred did not want to get wet unless absolutely necessary. They had determined, through visual and verbal evidence provided by the two copulators, that this was not a rape, but merely a misdemeanor lewd conduct violation. Since there were no other people to witness the lewd act, the officers decided to get the lovebirds' attention and tell them to continue the consummation of their affection in a more discreet location.

Norm flashed the high beams. Fred hit them with the spotlight. Norm hit the car's horn and then flicked the siren for a few seconds. None of this caused the lovemaking to stop or even induced the slightest disruption in the rhythmic slapping of flesh against flesh in the water. Having no other choice, Fred and Norm jumped out of their police car and stood over the writhing passion exhibition. They coughed, cleared their throats, and finally Norm kicked the man's naked derriere in the middle of a plunging stroke. This caused the man to lose concentration. He finally looked up and saw the two uniformed police officers. He immediately staggered to his feet and attempted to stand at attention.

This was difficult because of his inebriated state. He then looked down at his co-violator, who was laying splay-legged in the running water, muttering, "Don't stop. Don't stop."

The male suspect then nudged the female suspect with his foot and yelled, "Get up. Get up, you bitch, and show some class."

Part 5: Back to Patrol from Juvenile

Section 1: Cases

1: Losing a Court Case

One late afternoon on Watch III, Fred and I were dispatched to Recreation Park on a complaint of indecent exposure. When we arrived, there was a group of five or six teenage girls, between the ages of 13 and 16, waiting for us. One of them was the daughter of one of our dispatchers, Barbara. The girls told us that a white male in his twenties was riding his bicycle around the park. He was wearing a T-shirt and Dolphin shorts. The first time he rode past them, he just smiled. The second time, his smile was wider and the girls told us that his penis was hanging out the bottom of his shorts. They said that the suspect would keep riding past them, and his penis was always hanging out the bottom of his shorts. On at least one of these occasions, he actually put his hand down and rubbed his penis.

As we were talking to these victims, one of the girls pointed up Federation Drive and said, "There he goes now!" She was pointing to a man matching the description they had given. He had made a U-turn and was riding his bicycle away from us. He was about 50 yards away and we yelled for him to stop, which he did. While approaching the suspect, we explained the procedure for making a private person's arrest. After one of the girls made the arrest, we handcuffed the suspect and put him in the back of our patrol car. We wrote down the information we needed for our report.

En route to the station, Fred advised the suspect of his rights, which he waived. He denied purposefully exposing himself to the girls, but granted that his penis may have inadvertently slipped out of the bottom of his shorts while he was riding his bike past them. We booked him, wrote our reports and went back into service.

A few months after this incident, Fred and I were both subpoenaed to Municipal Court. The City Prosecutor decided to have the girls each testify first, before calling Fred and me. After the third or fourth girl testified, the City Prosecutor came out in the hallway. He was laughing and shaking his head. As he approached us, he said, "I'm sorry. You guys can go. We lost this case." We were a little puzzled until he explained.

The last girl who testified stated on direct examination that she saw the defendant, who she identified, riding his bicycle toward her and her friends. She stated that his penis was hanging out of his shorts. On cross examination, the defense attorney asked her how far the defendant's penis was sticking out the bottom of his shorts. The young witness asked him what he meant and the lawyer said, "Well, was it sticking out one or two inches from the bottom of his shorts?" The witness looked at the defendant, then back at the attorney and said, "It was hanging out about 25 inches from his shorts!"

There was laughter from everyone in the courtroom, including the jury.

The prosecutor told us he could barely restrain himself from standing up and telling the court, "Your honor, this man is innocent, but I would like to plead guilty to this offense!" The judge, prosecutor, and defense attorney agreed to dismiss the charges after agreeing that the girl's testimony had prejudiced the case against the prosecution!

2: Bank Robber in Bell Gardens

After an officer had been on a year or so, he or she was allowed to pick the partner they would like to work with. Often, officers chose someone who had been in their Police Academy class. Sometimes, however, you would get better days off working with a senior officer. Usually, one preferred a partner with a compatible personality. Once in a while a cop would have to change from a really good partner to adjust his schedule to get more time at home with a working spouse or for child care reasons. If an officer found himself working with a partner with whom he could not get along, he usually notified his sergeant and found a new partner. I only had to do this once in my career. After just one night with this guy, I found him to be arrogant, obnoxious, heavy handed and, how can I put this diplomatically, a real prick. At the end of the shift, I went to the sergeant and told him to never put me with that guy again. The sergeant obliged me.

During my years working as a patrol officer, I worked with several partners. Some were senior to me like Dick, Tom, and Fred. Some of us had about the same seniority like Doug and Dennis. On patrols, the partners I worked with the longest had a few years less seniority, like Steve, Bob and—my longest partnership—Norm. Norm had been hired on Long Beach Police Department under a special program. When the funds ran out for that program, Norm and several other officers were laid off. Norm was soon hired by Bell Gardens PD.

Eventually, Norm was rehired by Long Beach and we worked together again. He told me about an experience he had had while patrolling the streets of Bell Gardens. (All first responders, and police officers in particular, develop a "gallows humor" that others may find a little sick. Occasionally, during the course of a dangerous or even tragic incident, someone, usually an unsuspecting citizen, will do something so obviously stupid that it may cause their own injury or that of another. Police officers sometimes find humor in these dangerous situations. This is one of those occurrences.)

Bell Garden PD apparently works one-man cars. Norm was working day patrol when he heard another unit dispatched to an "Armed 211 Now" (robbery at a bank). Norm radioed that he would cover the back of the bank. He drove into the back parking lot, grabbed his shotgun, jacked a round into the chamber, and positioned himself, using his patrol car for cover. Since the bank had glass walls in the front and the back, Norm was able to see his fellow patrol officer get out of his patrol car in the front of the bank. Norm also saw the robber exit the front door, and upon seeing the police officer, fire a shot in his direction. To Norm it looked like the other officer was hit and went down. Thankfully, the other officer was just ducking for cover.

The robber decided that his escape from the front door was no longer safe, so he turned around and headed to the back door. Norm was standing behind his car, about 15 to 20 feet from the rear door of the bank. Before the robber came out, a clueless citizen tapped Norm on the shoulder and said, "Hey, man, you're blocking my car. I can't get out." As Norm grabbed the citizen to pull him behind the car, the robber came out the back door and let loose a round at Norm. Unfortunately for the hapless citizen, he was the one the bullet hit, and he went down.

Norm turned and fired the shotgun, hitting the bank robber. Norm told me that he thought he had shot the head off the robber! It was later discovered that the robber had been wearing a disguise that included a hat over a wig. Norm saw what he thought was the robber's head flying away from his body, but it was merely the hat and wig. Regardless, the robber was fatally wounded. The citizen recovered from his gunshot wound and, hopefully, he learned that he shouldn't approach a police officer who is pointing a weapon toward a bank!

3: Purse Snatcher's Surprise

It is always good to have a regular partner. You know his or her personality and work methods. That being said, even with a regular partner, a street cop will occasionally work with other cops when the partner is off on a holiday or vacation, sick or injured. When a cop's partner is off for more than one shift, the officer will probably work with a different partner every night. That is because on any particular shift, officers will be off for a variety of reasons and the scheduling sergeant has to fill in every beat with the personnel that are available. One night when Norm had a holiday, I was assigned to work with a younger officer, Dan, who was only recently off probation. At that time, a rookie was on probation for a year after his hire date. That meant that while he was on probation he could be fired, and his dismissal was not subject to Civil Service review.

Dan was enthusiastic, personable, and talkative. We were dispatched right out of the station on a purse snatching report. When we arrived at the scene, the paramedics were working on the victim who had broken her arm when she fell while the suspect was pulling her purse away. Although she was in some pain, the victim was able to relate what happened. Despite her discomfort, the victim started giggling when she told us her story. Dan, the paramedics, and I joined in on the laughter when she told us what had occurred.

It seemed that she bought the purse at a secondhand shop for twenty-five cents. She did not use that purse to carry her wallet or any other valuables. She used it to pick up her dog's poop (her word) in the vacant lot down the street from her apartment. She had walked her basset hound earlier in the day, but had forgotten her purse. Leaving her dog back in her apartment, the victim grabbed her purse and walked back to the vacant lot to pick up her hound's droppings.

After depositing her dog's crap and that of some other dog's business into the purse, she snapped it shut. She had started walking back home when the suspect came running up behind her. He grabbed the purse and yanked it, breaking the strap and causing the victim to fall to the ground, fracturing her left arm. She started tittering again when she said, "It would all be worth it if I could have seen his face when he opened that purse and saw what he had really stolen!"

4: Citizen's Request

One time, Norm and I were dispatched to a Winchell's on a "415 customer," which means a patron who is causing a disturbance. Dana was the counter girl on this particular evening and she was working by herself. A female in her early thirties, who had been drinking, came into the Winchell's and began yelling and screaming. Dana told her she had to leave. The obstreperous customer refused. When we arrived, we talked the female outside, but she said she would go back in when we left.

One of a patrol officer's greatest joys is kissing off a troublesome citizen to his or her sergeant. We asked her if she would wait outside until our sergeant arrived, so she could tell him what was causing her angst. The rambunctious citizen agreed to wait outside until the sergeant arrived. We then went to a clear channel on the radio with Sergeant Dave, who was single and quite the ladies' man, and told him that a female wanted to meet him outside the Winchell's at Stearns and Palo Verde. He gave us an ETA of five minutes, so we told the woman to stay right where she was until Sergeant Dave arrived.

We then got into our squad car and found a suitable hiding place to watch Sergeant Dave's suave moves. Veteran that he was, however, Sergeant Dave knew exactly what we were doing. Also, he had already had contact with the customer the night before, at the bar across the street from the Winchell's. When he arrived, Sergeant Dave ordered us to return to the donut shop. When we got back, in addition to giving us the evil eye, he chewed us out for not properly handling the call. So we talked to the uncooperative woman and told her that if she went back into Winchell's, we were going to arrest her. At first, she started walking toward the front door of the donut shop, but then, when she saw that we were following her, she would stop.

Finally, she turned toward us and said, "Well, if I can't go into the donut shop, I'm going over to that bar." She pointed to the drinking establishment across Stearns Street, where Sergeant Dave had seen her the night before. Norm and I thought this was a great idea and told her to go ahead. Sergeant Dave, however, told us that this was a bad idea, since the night before this individual had been 86'd forever from that bar. We then told her that she couldn't go to the bar either, that she had to go home. The woman suddenly threw a temper tantrum, threw herself to the asphalt parking lot, lifted her skirt to where it became obvious that she had gone "commando," and started yelling, "Fuck me, then. Fuck me right here."

Norm and I started laughing, and Norm, in his own inimitable style, turned to Sergeant Dave and asked, "Sergeant Dave, do I have permission to fulfill the citizen's request?"

Sergeant Dave flinched, replying, "God, no. Don't even say that. If anybody hears that we'll be in deep shit." It was evident that this woman was intoxicated so we handcuffed her. As we were putting her in the car, Sergeant Dave said, "Hold on. I'm having a female go with you guys." He ordered the unit with Debby and her partner to assist us. Debby got into the back of my squad car with the woman and I got into Debby's car with her partner. While driving to the station, Norm pulled over to the side of the San Diego Freeway and we followed suit. It turned out that the woman had bitten Debby on her hand, drawing blood. We wound up with a load of paperwork for a felony battery on a police officer, and Debby had to go the ER to get her wound cleaned and stitched.

5: Whoopee Cushion in the Homicide Car

I shot a burglar on Molino Avenue. I should have shot my partner, Norm. We were dispatched to the three or four hundred block of Molino on a "burglar there now" call. Usually, when we were near the scene, one of us said, "I'll take the front" or "I'll take the back." On this occasion, as we turned onto Molino, Norm declared, "You take the back. It's your turn."

I responded, "What do you mean, it's my turn to take the back?"

"I took the back last time," Norm said.

"Okay," I said, "I'll take the back." I didn't remember who took the back the last time we had a similar call. It just irritated me that Norm was so insistent that I take the back of the apartment. As I recall, it was apartment #4 that was being burglarized. This was a two story building that looked like it had eight units, four on the first floor and four on the second.

There was a concrete walkway between the rear of the building and a six-and-a-half foot grape stake fence. I started down this walkway toward the last set of windows, which I surmised was apartment 4. About halfway there, I heard Norm yelling, "He's coming out the back! He's coming out the back!" Unfortunately for me, the last set of windows was the laundry room. As I passed the second to the last set of windows, the suspect leaped out and landed on my back. I had my nightstick and my flashlight in my left hand and my .45 caliber service weapon in my right. When the suspect landed on my back, I was jolted and dropped my flashlight.

The suspect then jumped on the grape stake fence and tried to pull himself over it. I pulled him off the fence and pulled back my gun hand. The suspect grabbed my nightstick higher on the handle than I was holding it and hit me in the mouth with it, which forced me to let go. He held on to it and pulled it back and started to strike me again with it. I fired my weapon. The suspect took off toward the front of the building which was lit. I brought my gun up. The suspect was completely silhouetted.

Ten years earlier, if I had shot a burglar, I would have been given a day off with pay, but at that time, the DA would have most likely filed manslaughter charges against me. Before I was hired, the state law in California, as in most states, was that a police officer could shoot a fleeing felon. That was still the state law, but our department had a policy that an officer could only shoot a fleeing felon if the felon posed a deadly threat to the officer or other persons. So I didn't shoot a second shot, but started chasing the suspect, who turned and ran northbound on Molino like a bat out of hell. I thought, how did I miss the burglar when he was less than three feet away? Running northbound on Molino turned out to be a tactical error by the suspect. As I started running after the suspect, I heard Norm yelling, "Are you all right?" I answered that I was okay as I came out on Molino. Another unit, with Doug and Ron in it, had heard the shot and were heading southbound on Molino. They saw the suspect running northbound, jumped out of their car with their guns drawn and ordered the suspect to stop. He immediately made a U-turn and there I was pointing my .45 at him. I ordered him to the ground and he complied. I didn't see any blood, but I couldn't believe that I had missed him since we were so close to each other.

As I was handcuffing him, I asked if he had been shot. He told me he had. I asked him where he had been shot, and he said, "In my leg." Sure enough, there was a bullet hole in his pant leg with a little blood around it. We called for paramedics, a supervisor, and Homicide detectives, who handled all officer-involved shootings. We ran the suspect and the Nora (Narcotics) units told us that he was one of their informants.

The Homicide investigators who responded to the scene were John and Bill. John was upset because he and his wife had been out to dinner with some out of state cops, and he had been called away before he could eat. After running us through what had happened at the scene, they put Norm and me into the backseat of their plain car and started driving us to the station to take our written statements. It was getting late by this time and Norm and I had not eaten yet. Norm asked John if they would stop by one of the many hamburger stands on the way to the station so we could get our Code 7 (dinner). "No," John said. "I got pulled away from my dinner, so you guys don't need to eat either."

Norm looked over at me and smiled. He pulled out a Whoopee Cushion from his shirt and surreptitiously started blowing it up. Then he lifted up one cheek of his fanny and sat on it. It made a loud sound like someone passing gas after eating a bean and broccoli burrito. John turned around with a disgusted look on his face and asked, "What's the matter with you?"

Norm said, "I get this way when I'm hungry. You guys won't stop." Bill pulled into the next hamburger stand and Norm and I ordered our dinner.

6: Killing or Killing with Kindness

About midnight one night Bob and I were dispatched to an "unknown trouble call" of a woman screaming. It was from an address on Broadway, east of Redondo Avenue. The radio call said that it was coming from the apartment across the alley from the complaining party's (CP's) apartment. I drove the car slowly down the alley but neither Bob nor I heard anything. Suddenly a window opened from the two-story apartment building of the CP, which was on my side of the car. Across the alley was a three-story apartment. A middle-aged woman stuck her head out the window of the two-story apartment and told us, "It came from that building over there," pointing across the alley. I asked her what she heard and she stated, "It was a woman screaming and I thought someone was killing her."

A window opened on Bob's side of the car and another woman in the three-story building yelled at us that the screams had actually come from the two-story apartment. Another couple of windows opened on each side of the alley, with occupants pointing to the opposite apartment as the one that emitted the screams. Finally, a woman on my side of the alley told us that she used to live in the three-story apartment and that she thought the screams were coming from apartment number 310 or 312. I asked her what the screams sounded like, and she said, "You know what they sounded like." I told her that the original complaining party told us that it sounded like someone was killing the woman. This lady coughed a laugh and declared, "Yeah, killing her with kindness!" I then asked her if she was saying that she believed that this screaming was caused by a romantic encounter. She rather disrespectfully replied, "You've got it, Dick Tracy."

I parked the car and Bob advised Communications of the address where we were going. We went to the third floor and knocked on the door of Apartment 312. After hearing some rustling on the inside, the door opened and a little old lady about eighty years old, in a bathrobe, opened the door. She looked right at us and said, "It wasn't me, I live alone," and slammed the door in our faces.

We looked at each other, laughed and then walked over to Apartment 310. We didn't get an immediate answer, so we knocked again a little louder and yelled "Police."

After some rumblings inside, that door opened and a man about thirty opened the door and asked, "What seems to be the problem, Officers?" We told him that we were sent to check on a call about a woman screaming and asked if there was anyone else in the apartment. He stood a little straighter and puffed out his chest and with a roguish grin said, "Just my fiancé." An attractive young lady in her twenties, wearing a man's pajama top, peeked around the corner.

With a red face and an embarrassed smile she told us, "That was me. I get a little excited sometimes when we're in bed."

Wanting to get in the last word, Bob, trying to keep a straight face, giggled out, "Well, try and keep it down. Your neighbors were pretty concerned."

7: The Original Case of the Ass

While on patrol one night, Norm and I were dispatched to the Rusty Pelican on Marina Drive. There was supposed to be a major 415 (disturbance of the peace) fight. I was driving on Appian Way, which was through an upscale neighborhood. At that time, Bay Shore had a stop sign for those who wanted to enter Appian, but there was no stop sign on Appian Way at Bay Shore Avenue, so I was going pretty fast. We were about 100 yards from Bay Shore when a Porsche 914 entered the intersection and came to a complete stop in my lane. Since the Porsche had stopped, I started to go around the car on its left. The Porsche started forward again, right into my line of travel. I then attempted to go around the car on its right. Unfortunately, I had too much speed and we slid sideways into the side of the Porsche.

I thought we had killed the driver! Fortunately, we hit door to door and, while damaging both vehicles, the impact was spread over a larger area of both cars, resulting in our squad car merely pushing the Porsche about fifteen or so feet down the road. Norm had banged his knee into the shotgun and was hurting. As he climbed out of the squad car, he called for a supervisor and for paramedics. I couldn't open my car door, so I had to crawl over the center and out the passenger door. As I was crawling out, I smelled something and thought, "apple blossoms? No that smells like... Mace!" I looked down and saw that my can of Mace was crushed, and I realized the left cheek of my fanny felt like it had caught fire!

Norm had limped over and found out that the driver of the Porsche was uninjured, so he canceled the paramedics. I saw a garden hose at the corner house. I ran over there, turned on the hose, and ran it on the outside of my pants. In retrospect, I should have put the hose inside my pants to wash the mace off my left cheek. Instead it just pushed it more into my skin, but the water was cold and it seemed to stop the fire on my butt.

By the time I was done, Lieutenant Howard and Sergeant Todd were at the intersection, along with the patrol unit that had arrived to take the collision report. Norm was talking to the LT and the sergeant, asking them if they could get a unit to take him to Community Hospital to check out his knee. As usually happens when cops get in a car wreck, units came by to rag on the driver. The LT ordered one of them to take Norm to the hospital. After Norm left, the burning heat returned to my posterior, and I told Lieutenant Howard and Sergeant Todd. Just then, another squad car drove up with Doug and Hernando laughing at me. The lieutenant told them to stop and ordered them to take me to the hospital, too.

As I got into their car, I ripped off my gun belt and pulled down my pants and underwear while I told Doug and Hernando about the Mace. As we were driving, they both started whining about their eyes stinging. I told them I didn't feel the least bit sorry for them. They had come by to laugh at me and this was what they deserved.

At the hospital emergency room, I was taken to a room with a gurney that was separated from the next gurney by a curtain. Norm was on that gurney, but he didn't see me. Some of the nurses we knew, from the times we spent taking and filing reports there, came in to laugh and make snide remarks to me, including Tom, a gay male nurse. I don't know what the nurses put on my fanny, but it instantly put the fire out on my left cheek.

They gave me a set of scrubs to wear. Norm still didn't know I was so close, so I quietly asked one of the nurses to get me a surgical mask and cap, which she did. After donning my scrubs, mask and cap, I went through the curtain, holding my hands up, and said, "Is dis patient reddy for surgery?" Norm started yelling at his nurse for her to get "that psycho out of my room."

By the time the Doc had x-rayed and checked out Norm knee, it was EOW (End of Watch) and another unit gave us a ride to the station.

They put my uniform in the trunk.

We had the next three days off. When I returned to work, Norm was IOD (Injured On Duty) and off a few days. I worked the next four days with a different partner every night. That Saturday was the Long Beach Grand Prix and I was scheduled to work two eight-hour overtime shifts. I put on the uniform that I had picked up at the cleaners. While my left fanny cheek hadn't hurt at all since the nurses had put out the fire, the skin had turned pink, like a sunburn. About halfway through my first overtime shift, my left fanny cheek started itching. I thought that it was probably starting to peel, like a sunburn. In the locker room, after my second shift, I took off my uniform pants and pulled down my boxer shorts to see if my burn was healing. I was shocked to see that the area that had been pink was now a bright red, puffy and wrinkly like elephant skin! I went to the City Health Doctor the next day and he placed me on IOD for five working days. He told me I couldn't wear clothing for a week and prescribed a silver-based crème to rub on the affected area. This was the only time in my 29-year police career that I was IOD.

8: Report Writing

While most police officers' least favorite part of the job is writing reports, I understood it was an essential part of the job. I remember telling rookies that, while the guns on their hips might actually be fired once or twice in a career, and their handcuffs will subdue many a bad guy, the pen in their shirt pockets would put more crooks in jail for longer periods than any other "weapon" at their disposal. On many occasions, reports can be fun to write.

One summer night I was working with Tim. Tim is big guy with a sick sense of humor, which is why we get along so well. Early in our shift, while it was still daylight, we were dispatched to Recreation Park on a fight. When we arrived, we didn't see anyone throwing punches, but we were approached by a skinny, long haired, white male in his late twenties. He pointed at another white male subject who was about six feet, five inches and weighed about 280 pounds. "That guy grabbed my dick while I was taking a leak in the men's room. He said he wanted to go down on me. I told him 'no' but he keeps following me around the park and won't leave me alone. I've been yelling at him, but he keeps coming back."

Tim told him that this was a crime and that the guy could go to jail. Tim explained that the crime was a misdemeanor, not committed in our presence, so he, the hippie-looking victim, would have to place the suspect under "private person's arrest." The victim stated, "Yeah, I want him to go to jail, man. He grabbed my dick."

I distinctly heard Tim tell the victim that we would walk over with him to the suspect and that he should say, "You are under arrest for lewd conduct." I walked over to the suspect, who was standing next to the men's room. I told him we were sent to the park on a fight call and asked him what had occurred.

He told me that he and the hippie were just yelling at each other but that no one had gotten physical. He pointed out his size as opposed to the hippie's, and said that if there had been a fight he would have ended up the victor. He denied that he had purposefully touched the victim in his private area, but conceded that he might have "accidentally brushed up against him."

I motioned to Tim. He and the victim walked up to us and the victim blurted out, "You're under arrest, motherfucker, for attempting to suck my dick." After Tim and I stopped laughing and handcuffed the suspect, we advised the victim to tell the suspect he was under arrest for lewd conduct, which he did. We put both statements in the Arrest Report and we heard that the report made it all around the City Prosecutor's Office.

9: Nobody's Gonna Punk Me

Another time, my partner Steve and I were filing a report at St. Mary's Hospital near the Emergency Room when another unit came into the ER. They had a robbery suspect in custody who had inadvertently stabbed himself in the process of stabbing his victim. The suspect would need to be looked at and sutured by the ER doc. The ambulance was just bringing in the victim, who had multiple stab wounds. The officers in this unit asked us if we could watch their suspect while they spoke to the victim, in order to get his information to file their crime report.

The suspect, who was strapped to a gurney, was young. I asked him how old he was. In typical hoodlum fashion he said, "Fuck you, motherfucker." The male nurse told us that the information they had was that he was 19 years old. "That's right, motherfucker."

I became slightly irritated, not so much by his attitude; that I expected. What bothered me was his lack of a vocabulary beyond the F word or its derivatives. So I decided to play with his feeble mind. "OOOH! Nineteen," I said. "We've got your knife, we have the victim's statement, we have the witnesses' statements. You'll be going to prison for this robbery. They're going to love a nice skinny kid like you, with a nice round butt. Some big ugly Bubba is going to get a hold of you and butt fuck you into a coma."

"Nobody's gonna punk me," the suspect adamantly told us and he kept repeating it numerous times, more stridently with each repetition. About that time, the male nurse returned to the examination room with a catheter. He unzipped the suspect's pants and pulled them and his underpants down. The suspect started struggling against his restraints and yelling, "What are you doing, man? Don't touch me." The male nurse responded, "The doctor ordered that you be catheterized." He then proceeded to put the catheter in. The big, tough suspect started to cry and mournfully whined, "I been punked. I been punked."

10: The Burglar's Surprise

Norm and I were working our patrol beat in East Long Beach when we received a call to meet Sergeant Todd at 4th Street and Temple. Sergeant Todd told us that the male black man he had been speaking with at the bus stop matched the description of a suspect who had been seen leaving the scene of a burglary in the Naples area of East Long Beach, three or four hours before. Naples is about two and a half miles away from the bus stop, but the burglar had escaped. The subject the Sarge was talking with appeared nervous. Sergeant Todd asked us to check out his story. The subject told us that he had been at his girlfriend's house, a block away from the bus stop. He said he had been there for about four or five hours, having dinner and watching a movie with his girlfriend and her mother. This subject had no ID, but gave us a name and date of birth. He gave us the address and apartment number of his girlfriend. I patted him down for weapons and told him to get in the back of our patrol car, which he did. It should be noted that once the back door of a patrol car is closed, it supposedly cannot be opened from the inside.

Norm drove the block to the girlfriend's apartment and I got out, went to the apartment, and knocked on the door. An attractive black female in her early twenties answered. Her mother was sitting on the sofa in the living room. When I asked them if they knew the subject, they didn't recognize the name he gave us. When I explained the circumstances, they told me that he was not the young lady's boyfriend, but was an acquaintance who had lived near them in their old neighborhood in central Long Beach. They gave me his correct name and told me that he had only been at their apartment for about an hour.

This ruined his alibi for the time of the burglary. I went back to our patrol car, and casually leaning in the passenger door, called the suspect by his correct name and told him that we were calling the burglary witnesses to see if they could ID him. With that, he somehow opened the rear driver's side door and took off running westbound across Temple and in between houses. I took off on foot after him. Norm drove the car around the block. When I got to the next street, I saw our patrol car stopped in the middle of the street, with the engine running, and the driver's side door open. I knew that Norm had seen the suspect, stopped the patrol car, and taken up a foot pursuit.

I hopped in the driver's seat and drove around to the next block west, which was the direction the suspect had been going. I slowed when I got to the middle of the block where I thought the suspect had gone. As I slowed, I could hear Norm yelling, "Buz, he's back here." I pulled our car into the driveway, got out and ran toward the backyard, where Norm was still yelling. This house was U-shaped and Norm was standing in the middle of the U.

"The suspect's somewhere in here. I dropped my flashlight. See if you can see him." At this point, I saw a family—a mom, dad and two kids—looking out a window.

The father said, "It sounded like he went into those bushes." He pointed at some large bushes planted in a flower bed.

I pointed my flashlight at the base of the bushes and we saw the prone body of the suspect. We both had our guns pointed toward the suspect, and Norm immediately yelled, "Don't move." When he yelled, the suspect swiftly attempted to jump up. Norm fired one shot and the suspect fell right to the ground and started groaning.

As Norm was calling for the paramedics, Homicide investigators and a supervisor, I went down into the bushes, handcuffed the moaning suspect, and pulled him out of the flowerbed and onto the concrete. I didn't notice any pool of blood in the flowerbed or any blood smears on the concrete. "Did you get shot?" I asked.

"Yeah" the crook said.

"Where?" I asked.

“In my tummy.” replied the bad guy.

I rolled him on his right side and looked at his stomach. I didn’t see any bullet holes or blood and I told him, “You’re not hit!”

The suspect, still moaning and groaning told me, “The other side.”

I rolled him on his left side and again there were no bullet holes. “You’re not hit you big....” I refrained from calling him a pussy, wimp or asshole, as the family was still there looking at us through their open window.

We later determined that Norm had shot at the suspect as he was jumping up, Norm’s bullet had hit the dirt just below him, causing dirt to fly up and hit the suspect in his belly. This caused him to think he had been shot!

When the supervisor, Sergeant Todd, arrived, he canceled Homicide since this was a non-hit shooting. Several units arrived to assist. Jake and his partner volunteered to take the suspect to booking. Jake was one of our black police officers, and having him transport the black suspect to Booking would minimalize the likelihood of any charges of racist brutality while driving the suspect to the station.

Norm told Sergeant Todd that he had knocked down the back alley fence when chasing the suspect who had just jumped over it. He told the Sarge and me that, after he saw the suspect grab the fence and vault over it, Norm thought, this is just like the wall at the academy. So as he ran up to the redwood fence, he grabbed the top, planted his foot in the middle, and before he could pull himself over, the whole fence came down. We told the family that the city would pay for the downed fence and I believe they did. After going over the whole incident with the Sergeant, we drove back to the station to file our reports.

In Reporting, Jake and his partner came into the room. Jake had a sour look on his face and sarcastically said, “Thanks a lot, you guys!” We asked him what was wrong and Jake told us that the suspect had crapped his pants. Norm and I laughed and thanked Jake and his partner for going above and beyond the call of duty. Norm had literally scared the shit out of this burglar!

Section 2: Pranks

1: Fred and the Radio

After working the J-cars and Juvenile Detectives for about three years, I felt it was time to go back to Patrol and work on the streets. (A couple of new recruit classes had come through training and they were being rotated into working the Booking Desk, Communications, the jail and the Front Desk.)

For the first eight months back on Patrol I had to work the Graveyard shift. It seemed like five years. I could never get used to staying awake all night and sleeping during the day. I had a good partner on Graveyard, but the hours were killing me. I was finally able to get to my preferred shift, Watch III, nights.

When handheld radios became the latest technology, they were very expensive. The City of Long Beach only budgeted for a limited number, which meant that only one radio was assigned to each two-man unit. On one particular night, Fred, my old Juvenile partner, and I were working together in a squad car assigned to Unit 2 Charlie 11, and Fred was carrying the radio. We were dispatched to a motel in our beat regarding loud music. We parked in the motel parking lot and heard some music playing that wasn't especially loud. As we were walking through the lot, I saw a newer car and told Fred to give me the handheld. "I want to run that license plate."

Fred looked at the car, read the plate, and then put a death grip on the radio. Fred looked me straight in the eye and said, "Aw, naw, you are not runnin' that plate."

When we were walking back to our car after advising the music player to turn it down a little, I pulled the radio from Fred's belt, keyed the mic and said in my best Dutch accent, "Two Charles Elephen."

The dispatcher replied, "Two Charlie Eleven, go ahead."

Continuing in my role as Fred, I added, "Charlie Elephen, we advise, 10-8 (meaning we were back in service, available for calls) and I would like a 28 and 29 (meaning the registered owner and any wants or warrants) on California personal plate RED DICK that's Robert, Edward, David, David, Ida, Charles, King."

The female dispatcher, Barbara, I think, just repeated the phonetic spelling without using my Dutch accented separation of the name into two words.

A minute later, Barbara came back on the radio, in a voice dripping with sarcasm, "Your plate comes back to a last of Reddick, first of Thomas, who lives at.... No wants or warrants."

In character, I responded, "Oh, Ahm sorry, I guess I mispronounced the name. 10-8."

As I handed the radio back to Fred, he said, "You son of bitch. Now everyone will think it was me."

As we got back into our black and white I told him, "Don't worry, Fred, they'll get over it."

2: Donut Dust

It's hard to remember what started our feud with Doug and Ron, who worked an adjoining unit to Fred and me. At any rate, they had done something that provoked us, and we came up with a plan for our revenge. That same Winchell's was at the corner of Anaheim and Ximeno. Fred and I often drank coffee or hot chocolate there while we filed reports. We asked one of the girls who worked there if we could buy a couple of cups of the flour they used to make donuts. She gave us two plastic baggies full of the donut dust (and refused payment). All Fred and I had to do was wait for the proper time and think of a good technique to place this flour into the air conditioner ducts in Doug and Ron's black and white.

After brainstorming between calls for service, Fred and I came up with the best way to put the flour in the air ducts. Our plan was to take a "hot sheet" (a hot sheet was a stiff piece of paper that had all of the license numbers of the stolen cars in the city), form it into a cone, place the small end of the cone into the duct and pour the flour into the large end of the cone.

When we weren't answering our own calls, we were surreptitiously following Doug and Ron on their calls. Unfortunately, they always stayed within sight of their black and white on the three or four calls we were able to watch them.

Then our luck changed—for the worse. Doug and Ron arrested a wino for being drunk in public. It wasn't a busy night, so we waited a while until Fred and I figured they were done booking their prisoner. We drove into the booking tunnel and found their car, which was parked in the first space, adjacent to the glass doors to the Booking Desk and the jail elevator. Doug and Ron were no longer at the Booking Desk, so we figured we could get in their car, pour the donut dust into the air ducts, and turn their air and fan to full blast. When they started their car, it would blow a fine white flour all over their blue wool uniforms.

We parked our car several parking spaces away and ran to Doug and Ron's squad car. It was unlocked (but that didn't matter anyway since, at that time, all the police cars were keyed the same). Fred got in on the driver's side and immediately turned on the fan and air since the engine wasn't on. I coned my hot sheet and started pouring copious amounts of flour in the vent on the passenger side. Fred was giggling like a schoolgirl, and most of his flour wound up on the floor of the squad car. Just as I finished my baggie of flour, I looked up and saw Doug and Ron coming out of the jail elevator. I told Fred and he looked up just as Doug and Ron realized we were in their car. Fred grabbed his keys and started their car in an attempt to get away. Of course, when it started, the full force of the flour-filled vent covered me with donut dust! Since Fred had missed getting most of his flour in his vent, he was relatively unpowdered. Doug, Ron, the Booking Desk crew, and all the cops booking prisoners at the time were howling at me. In abject humiliation, Fred and I returned to our car.

3: Revenge of the Donut Dust

A few weeks later, when we least expected it (which is the key to a successful revenge prank), Doug and Ron extracted their revenge on our unsuccessful donut dust caper. We had a ride-along, Tom, who worked at El Castillo Real Restaurant, so naturally we went there for Code 7 (dinner). After the excellent dinner that one would always get at El Castillo's, we traipsed to the front of the establishment where our patrol car was parked. Our ride-along let himself into the backseat while Fred got into the driver's seat. I had snagged a sucker from the jar that was in front of the cash register and was standing next to the open passenger door, taking off the plastic wrapper, when Fred started the car.

I remember thinking that our car's air conditioner must be awfully cold because it looked like frost was coming out of the vents. Fred screamed while he was attempting, unsuccessfully, to turn off the air. He finally turned off the ignition and the stream of white flour stopped blowing on his navy blue uniform!

At that point, we heard screeching tires, raucous laughter, and the quick bleep of a police siren as a squad car across the street took off. Because I was still trying to take the wrapper off of my sucker, I was spared the indignity of having to extensively brush the flour off of my uniform. We did have to go back into El Castillo to get some towels for Fred's uniform and the inside of our patrol car. Doug and Ron had pulled off a very productive revenge prank, although Fred and I didn't think it was very original.

4: Assisting the Donut Queen

One night, my partner and I went into the Winchell's Donuts on Palo Verde and Stearns to file a report and get a cup of coffee. While my partner was filing his report over the phone, I was watching Linda, the chief donut maker and counter girl, making fresh donuts. She had already plunged the donuts in the hot oil and was turning them with what looked like chopsticks. Every time she turned one of the donuts, I noticed that Linda would wince as if the act was causing her pain. Linda was a well endowed woman of modest height, with a friendly personality, and I hated to see her in any discomfort. So I asked if she was all right. She told me that her back was killing her, and every time she rotated a donut she got a shooting pain in her lower back. Then I asked her if she wanted her back "cracked."

Linda asked me what that was. I told her that I would pick her up from behind by her elbows and give her a little jolt that would align her spine and therefore ease her back pain. Linda asked me if I had ever done this before and I told her that I had done it "hundreds of times." (In reality, I had only done it once or twice, but I had seen my dad perform the procedure several times.) Apparently the pain was so much for Linda that she agreed to have me crack her back. She asked me what she had to do and I told her to put her right hand on her left shoulder and her left hand on her right shoulder. By this time my partner had finished his report and was watching us with undisguised curiosity.

I came up behind Linda and grabbed her elbows. I lifted her off the ground and let her bounce in the air one time. Linda immediately screamed and ran directly to the ladies' room, which was about 10 feet in front of her. My partner and I looked at each other in total surprise and waited for Linda to return.

After a minute or so, a red-faced Linda came out of the ladies' room. We asked her what was wrong, and she told us, "I'm wearing a front snapping bra and when you did that it went twang and opened up!"

5: Imitating the Chief

Until a few weeks before the next incident, the Chief of Police had a radio call sign of "Command One." The Deputy Chiefs were "Command Two" and "Command Three," and the Captains went from "Command Four" to "Command Eight" or so, then Lieutenants went on as Command whatever their number of seniority was. When we heard the patrol lieutenants using the call signs of "Edward Nine" or "Edward Ten," we just thought that the Department had changed the lieutenants' call signs and apparently no one sent my partner—who at that time was Steve—and me the memo about the change from "Command" to "Edward."

At any rate, Steve and I had booked a prisoner in our jail, filed our reports, and returned to our squad car in the booking tunnel. Steve was driving and there was another black and white ahead of us waiting to get out of the tunnel. As we were sitting there waiting, Bobby got out of the car ahead of us. He walked over to a portable stop sign that had a hundred-pound cement base. Bobby dragged it over in front of our police car and left it there. He returned to his police car and hopped into the passenger seat as his partner, David, drove off.

This irritated me, since I then had to get out of my passenger seat and move it so that Steve could drive our cop car out of the tunnel. I thought, "Why should I be the only one to have the pleasure of dragging that heavy stop sign?" So after Steve drove past, I dragged the sign to the same position so that the next car that was going to leave would have to haul it out of the way. When I returned to my passenger seat, I looked over at Steve, "We ought to get on the radio, say we were one of the lieutenants, and order those guys to return to the station and move the stop sign out of the way."

Steve said, "Good idea," grabbed the mic, and threw it to me.

Not one to duck a challenge, I accepted the mic. Dave and Bobby worked in Area One and we worked in Area Two, so we were on two different frequencies. Also, I knew that the Area Two lieutenant's call sign was Edward Ten, so I thought that the Area One lieutenant's call sign would be less than that. I changed our radio to channel one, keyed the mic, and said, "Edward One."

The dispatcher immediately responded with, "Edward One, go ahead."

In my most official voice I said, "Edward One, have the unit with Officers David and Bobby return to the station and remove the stop sign they placed in the middle of the booking tunnel."

As the dispatcher was relaying this message, we parked our police car and hid outside the exit to the booking tunnel so we could see when Bobby and David returned and moved the stop sign. When they did, we heard another officer, who was nicknamed "Lizard," tell Bobby, "That didn't sound like Edward One to me. That sounded like Buz Williams."

I thought, "Lizard, you rat bastard, stop snitching me off."

David told Lizard. "Well, they told us it was Edward One, so we're moving it." After they moved the sign so that other cars could go by, David and Bobby hopped into their police car and started driving back to their beat.

We hopped into our car and were about to pull up next to them when David asked the dispatcher, "Who's the personnel in Edward One?"

The dispatcher's responded immediately, "That's the Chief of Police."

We quickly backed off. I decided that I didn't want anyone to know that I had imitated the Chief of Police on the police radio. After a few weeks with no repercussions, I may have impersonated the Chief again once or twice. Unfortunately, other officers did this, too, but I was getting the blame for it. I know for a fact that a couple of graveyard officers, Ray and Al, impersonated the Chief more than once, and some of the other cops were asking me if I was responsible. The ultimate result was that the Department started putting "G-Star" devices on the radios to determine which units were broadcasting.

6: Happy Birthday, Sarge

Most of the time when I worked with Norm, our sergeant was a big, loud, boisterous guy named Davy. He was a good guy to work for in Patrol. If you screwed up, he let you know in no uncertain terms, but he did it without an audience of other cops or citizens. Our working theory was that it was better to ask forgiveness than permission. So we pretty much did things our own way until Davy chewed us out and told us otherwise. After the Department put the G-Stars on the radios, imitating the Chief was curbed.

One day, as we started our shift, Norm told me that Davy's birthday was this particular day. Norm then suggested that I should, as Edward One, go to a clear channel on the radio with Davy and wish him a "fine, fine, fine" birthday. (The Chief had a habit of using the phrase "fine, fine, fine" when speaking.) By this time,

I had heard Norm on several occasions tell our fellow officers that if I ever made Chief of Police, Norm would be a Deputy Chief within a week, with all of the "dirt" he had on me. This caused me some angst, so I told Norm that if we could find a radio without a G-Star, I would start the radio transmission, but he would have to finish it.

Norm agreed and, before clearing a report call we were on, Norm drove to the station. We found an unlocked car with a stationary radio in it. Since that car radio had not logged on at the beginning of the shift, the Communication dispatchers would not know who was broadcasting. Norm pointed our squad car toward the exit of the police parking lot for a quick escape. I turned on the radio and said in my deepest voice, "Edward One." Then I threw the mic at Norm as the dispatcher replied, "Edward One, go ahead."

Norm then responded, "Can I go to a clear channel with Sergeant Davy?"

The dispatcher then commanded, "Sam One, channel four with Edward One."

Norm turned the radio to channel four and kept saying, "Sam One, Sam One, Sergeant Davy are you there?" Sergeant Davy never answered on channel four, so Norm turned back to our regular channel and said, "Edward One, Sergeant Davy is not responding, but when he gets back on the air, please advise him that I hope he has a fine, fine, fine birthday."

We then hopped back into our squad car and Norm, who had been a race car driver, hauled ass down Broadway.

Before we got to Alamitos, we heard Sam One ask the dispatcher, "What's Charlie Nine's 10-20 (location)?"

When the dispatcher asked us for our location, I paused a couple extra seconds, giving Norm time to get closer to our beat, before I answered, "We're just turning down the east/west alley between Ocean and 1st Street east of Junipero, as per a district car check from Sergeant Todd." By the time I had finished, Norm was just turning down the mouth of that alley. From the other end of that alley, we saw the lights of another black and white coming rapidly at us. Norm stopped our car and the other police car raced up and stopped right in front of us. It turned out to be Sergeant Davy. He jumped out of his car and ran to ours, pointing his flashlight in our windows.

Norm asked Davy what he was looking for and Davy replied, "You know what I'm looking for. I'm looking for the radio you used to call me claiming to be Edward One. I already called Communications and they said there was no G-Star on that transmission."

I worked up the most incredulous look I could conjure up and said to Norm, "I told you we would get blamed for that."

Norm turned back to Davy and asked, "Would you like to look in our trunk, Sarge? I'll pop it open for you."

Davy threw up his hands and exclaimed, "No, I don't want to look in your trunk. If you want me to look in your trunk I know the damned thing isn't in there."

Later that night we heard that Sergeant Davy had told several other officers that he had been sure that "Norm and Buz had been the ones imitating the Chief in wishing him a fine, fine, fine birthday, but they had been right where they said they were and only had the radios they had logged on with."

7: Flipping the Captain the Finger

A year or so later, I was working with Bob, and Sergeant Davy was still our Patrol Sergeant. One night about 1:30 AM, Bob was feeling sick. He went to a clear channel with Sergeant Davy and asked his permission to leave early. (Our EOW—End of Watch—was 2:30 AM and Dispatch usually started calling us out about 2:15 AM.) Sergeant Davy gave Bob permission and since I had a report to file, we drove to the station. Bob went home and I went to Reporting to file my report. I found an unoccupied steno and was able to dictate my report in about a third of the time it would have taken me to write it. I dawdled around at the station for a while, went down to the locker room and slowly changed out of my uniform. It was still only about 2AM, but I figured that I wouldn't get in any trouble leaving early since my partner was already gone.

I got into my personal car and started driving toward the exit of the parking lot where we parked our personal cars. As I approached the driveway exit, a patrol car parked next to the exit flashed on its high beams. I thought it was Sergeant Davy since I had caught a glimpse of only one person in the car, in the driver's seat. I figured that, since he knew my partner had gone home sick, he would know that it was pretty useless for me to go out for 15 minutes in a one-man car. So, as I drove up to the exit, I extended my middle finger to the occupant of the patrol car.

The next day, after the squad meeting, Sergeant Davy asked for a meeting with Bob and me. He told us we were in trouble for leaving early. Bob reminded the Sergeant that he had given Bob permission to leave his shift early, due to illness. Sergeant Davy then conceded that Bob was not in trouble, but that Captain George had wanted to fire me for insubordination. I asked, "Why, what did I do?" The sergeant told me that the Captain wanted me fired because I had flipped him the finger as I was driving out of the parking lot when I was leaving my shift early. I told Davy that I did not know it was the Captain. Davy told me that he told the Captain that I was a good cop, and had left early after I had finished filing a report and my partner had gone home sick. Sergeant Davy said he would chew me out, and the Captain agreed that would be the end of it. I thanked the sergeant profusely.

The aftermath of this event came a full twenty years later. About ten years after Sergeant Davy retired, and shortly after I retired, I ran into Davy at the Credit Union.

After reminiscing for a few minutes, I told Davy I had a confession to make. I then told him that it was Norm and me who had wished him a fine, fine, fine birthday back in the day. Davy laughed and then made his own confession. “Remember when I told you that you were in trouble for flipping Captain George the finger? That was me you actually flipped off!”

8: Partners in Love

Norm and I had gone Code 7 (out of service to eat) when Mark, one of the Training Officers on our watch, contacted us and asked if he and his rookie could eat with us. Mark introduced us to his young, attractive female rookie partner. They had been working together for a couple of weeks. Norm and I had begun to suspect that the closeness between this Rookie and her training officer might be a little more than just professional respect. The way they looked at each other and giggled at each other's silly jokes led us to this conclusion.

What happened while we were eating confirmed our suspicions. We were sitting in a booth when Mark and the Rookie came into the restaurant. I moved over and Mark sat next to me. Norm got up and let the Rookie sit across from me, and he sat opposite Mark. I saw the

Rookie reach under the table like she might be tying her shoe. A minute later a stocking foot started rubbing my thigh. I thought, "Oh, Buzzard, you've still got it." When I looked up, however, I saw that the Rookie was making eyes at Mark. I let her continue to rub my thigh for a few minutes and then grabbed her toe and moved her foot over to Mark's thigh and said, "I think your stroking the wrong thigh here, Rook." Mark and the Rookie blushed and giggled as Norm and I got up to go back to work.

9: A Honker on the Windshield

I had worked with both Bob and Steve as partners in squad cars, and both of them were good partners. Since I had four or five years seniority on them, they wanted to work together. So they partnered up. One night, while they were partners, they were driving out to their beat in East Long Beach from the downtown station. Bob was driving and Steve was in the passenger seat. Steve happened to be recovering from a cold. It was about 5 PM and they were traveling east on 7th Street, in rush hour traffic. Steve started coughing and choked up a golf-ball-sized hunk of slimy green snot. They were approaching a red light. Steve glanced to his right and, seeing no other vehicles, launched the huge green wad out the window.

Unfortunately, an affluent businessman in a brand new shiny Corvette was coming up in the lane next to their squad car and the snot ball's arc carried it to his windshield, right in front of the driver. Both cars had to stop for the red light. The businessman hit his windshield wipers, but all this did was spread the gelatinous goo over a wider part of his windshield. Steve turned to his partner and said, "Turn left. Get out of here." Bob, who was fully aware of what had occurred, told Steve that they were heading for their beat and he would not detour from their appointed rounds. Meanwhile, the offended citizen was glaring at Steve with a hate stare that could melt and boil ice cubes. Bob, being the dutiful responsive person he was, made it a point to stay next to the Vette and its vexed driver all the way to the on-ramp to the 405 and 22 freeways. All that time, Steve was calling Bob every obscene, raunchy, filthy name he could think of, while Bob placidly drove on, keeping pace with the Corvette and its fuming driver!

10: Communication Center Breaks Down

On occasion during my time on Watch III Patrol, when a training officer had a day off, I was assigned to train a rookie for a night or two. I happened to be training Robert one night. (This rookie, Robert, would later promote quite high in the Department.) A rookie is required to file all the reports, and Robert had taken all of the information to file a residential burglary report. It was approaching 7 PM and we hadn't eaten dinner yet, so when we got into our squad car, I grabbed the mic and said, "Charlie Nine, WFL (will file later), nine-twelve (can we go for dinner?)"

There was no response, so I repeated my first transmission. Still there was no response. I switched the radio from channel two to channel one, and broadcast, "Two Charlie Nine on one." There was still no response. I turned to my rookie, Robert, and declared, "Well, it looks like we're going to have a long, peaceful Code 7 (dinner) tonight," and I headed to El Castillo Real restaurant, which was on the border of our beat.

I realized I had left the radio on channel one when a voice came on and announced, "Charlie Three, we advise, 10-8" (back in service, available for dispatch).

The voice belonged to Joe, one of the Area One officers. Of course, Joe was also met with radio silence, so he repeated his transmission. After again receiving no response, Joe came back on the radio, and in a panicky voice squeaked out, "Charlie Three, can anyone out there hear me?"

I was still laughing at Joe when, a short time later, another voice came on channel one. "This is Sam Four" (the Area One Sergeant, Sergeant Charlie). He continued, "The Communication Center lost all power. I am driving the dispatchers over to Peterson Street. (Peterson Street was where the Fire Department had their Communications and we would use it in an emergency.) Our communications should be up and running in about a half an hour. Until then, you guys can talk car to car. You won't be getting dispatches for a while, so I suggest that you get with another unit and patrol with them until we can dispatch again."

This was music to my ears. This meant that the G-Stars were not working and there would be no way to know which unit was broadcasting. I grabbed my handheld radio, keyed the mic and said, "Edward One. I'm over here at the Communication Center. I seemed to have kicked a plug out of the wall." Hoops, hollers and catcalls followed from the other units!

11: Ski's Pictures of the Homeless

My first shift on a Grand Prix Saturday was with Ski, who worked the same afternoon shift I did. Ski had brought his small camera with him so he could take photos of the homeless, winos and derelicts that called downtown Long Beach their home. I don't know if Ski had a sociology class or was going to write a book, but he took some good photos. One man had wrapped himself in black plastic trash bags and was wearing spotless white gloves. As I recall, there was a sleeping wino with a bottle in a brown paper bag next to him. At any rate, Ski took several photos and then left his camera in the squad car when I dropped him off. My next partner for the night was a younger officer, John, who I had not worked with prior to that evening.

After about half an hour, John found Ski's camera between the front seats and asked if it was mine. I told him it was Ski's and that I would put it in his mailbox at the end of our OT shift. Then a brainstorm struck me and I told John to hand me the camera as I pulled to the curb. I held the camera so that it would only pick up my smiling face and not the uniform, and snapped the picture and advanced the film.

After taking the photo and putting the camera where I wouldn't forget it, John got an idea. He said, "Why don't you take a picture of your dick to leave on Ski's camera?" I dissuaded him from this folly by pointing out that he was a sick bastard for even thinking of such a prank, and even though I might think there was a touch of humor in it, I surely wouldn't take such a picture after photographing my face on the same roll of film.

A couple weeks later, after returning from my red ass injury, I was walking through the locker room. As I passed Ski's locker, he yelled, "Wait a minute, you lowlife dirtbag." I stopped and asked him what could possibly be the matter.

Ski said, "I got my pictures developed from the Grand Prix and brought them home. My wife knew I had taken pictures of some of our derelicts and she started looking through the photos. She pulled out one, and looked strangely at it, and asked me who this wino was. She showed it to me and I saw your smiling face." I told Ski he was extremely lucky it was the only picture I had taken!

12: Fingerprint Powder

Don was the main force behind the "I wear the world's smallest jock" prank against me so, of course, I vowed revenge. Don and I were working together after my previous partner, Norm, went to Detectives to work Vice. I have to say that Don was a very good, conscientious police officer. He had recently returned to Patrol after spending years working in the Narcotics Division. The first night we worked together, I realized that Don was an expert in narcotics enforcement, and had a superior knowledge of who was selling dope and where they were selling it.

That night, we secreted ourselves near a dope selling location, and Don spied through his binoculars. The next night I brought my binoculars, too. It didn't take long for me to realize that the binoculars presented a golden opportunity for me to mete out my revenge. I went to the

Crime Lab and obtained a small vial of black fingerprint powder. Early in our work shift, Don had to file a report at Community Hospital. I walked into the ER with Don, who went to the little reporting office we used there. When Don was in the middle of writing his report, I went out to our squad car, took the fingerprint powder, and rubbed it on the rubber eye pieces of Don's binoculars.

Later in the shift, we went out skulking with our binoculars. Apparently, I had inadvertently rubbed a little of the black powder on my cheek. Don saw it and told me about it. I said, "Humph, I wonder where that came from."

The plan worked perfectly. After using his binoculars, Don had big, black semicircles on the top half of his eyes. It looked as if he were wearing eye makeup. I didn't say a word.

We went to the Winchell's on 7th Street, just east of Redondo. As we were walking out with our coffee, a car pulled in next to our squad car and the passenger window came down. The young man, about twenty-five, looked like he was going to ask Don something, but stopped with his mouth agape and just stared at Don. Don looked back at me and then turned back to the young man and asked him, "Can I help you?"

The man slowly sputtered out, "Can you tell me how to get to Cal-State Long Beach from here?" Don told him, but the guy continued to stare at Don, slack-jawed.

Don, a little exasperated, rather abruptly inquired, "Is there anything else you need?"

The fellow said, "No, thanks," and rolled up his window as the driver headed toward Cal-State Long Beach.

"What was that guy's problem?" Don asked me.

"I don't know. Maybe he thought he knew you," I threw back at him. I was secretly laughing to myself because I knew that guy had never seen a male police officer with eye makeup before. Don really did look a little strange.

At EOW (end of watch), Don and I were walking toward the elevator in the station when my old partner, Steve, called out to Don. Both Don and Steve were on the SWAT team, and Steve wanted to know what time their training started the next day. Don turned around and Steve started asking, "What time is... ha, ha, when did you start wearing eye makeup?"

Don looked at me and I said, "Damn, it does look like you're wearing eye makeup."

Don's locker wasn't too far from mine and while we were getting out of our uniforms, Don yelled over to me, "Check your binoculars. That damn Steve put black powder on our eye pieces. That's where you got that smudge. I'll get back at him." Don made several witty flyers questioning Steve's masculinity, and the next day he put them all over the station. I was pretty proud that my prank had resulted in <u>two</u> victims!

13: Brown Bagus Short Dogus

I was working with an officer, Rob, who had two brothers in the Department. Rob and I were working our usual shift in East Long Beach when we were dispatched to a "man down" call in front of a market on East Anaheim Street. It was unusually slow in our beat because it was the weekend of the Long Beach Grand Prix, which was held in the downtown area. It was early in our shift, so it was still daylight when we pulled in front of the market. We saw one of the alcoholics that was forever going through the criminal justice system. He was laying on the sidewalk, passed out, holding a bottle of cheap wine in a paper bag.

After we threw away his half-consumed bottle, we were able to arouse him, determined that he was drunk in public, handcuffed him, and put him in the back of our police car. We drove to the station, walked our prisoner to the booking desk, and Rob started filling out the Booking Sheet that only had a few blank lines used as a short form for public intoxication.

As Rob was filling out the Booking Sheet, I suddenly realized that this was a golden opportunity to "wax poetic." I asked Rob if he had started the short form part of the sheet yet, and he told me he had not. I said, "give it to me." I filled in the short form with these words, "The above listed suspect was observed laying on the sidewalk with an empty bottle of Gallo Port at his side. This suspect was determined to be of the species indigenous to all metropolitan areas generically known as the Brown Bagus-Short Dogus, commonly called the downtown wino." We handed it to the Booking Sergeant, who gave it to one of the stenos. The suspect was booked in and we took our prisoner up to the 6th floor jail and went back to our beat.

A week later, Rob came into Squad Room and told me that I had gotten him in trouble.

"How?" I asked.

"The judge who read the short form drunk report at Municipal Court knows my brother Mike, who works Vice. He saw the last name of the reporting officer and thought he wrote the short form report. The judge started chewing Mike out and Mike told him he didn't write it, it was probably one of his brothers. Mike told the judge that he would take care of it. He called me and chewed me out and told me that the judge said that all you have to write is 'the suspect was intoxicated and unable to care for himself or others.'"

I still insist our report was more interesting.

14: Evidence

One of the most tedious reports to file is the Evidence Report. It is usually just property recovered at a crime scene, a search warrant location, or from a suspect. Each item has to be listed with a description, size, color, and serial number if it has one. As one would suspect, if there is a lot of evidence these reports can take hours.

One night, when Steve and I were partners, we were informed about a serial statutory rapist in a residential neighborhood. We had two or three girls aged 15 and 16 who were willing to come forward and ID the twenty-something suspect. They also informed us of a number of sex toys and pornography the suspect had in his house and garage. We went to see Jim, one of the sergeants in Narcotics, who assisted us in getting a search warrant for the suspect's house, car, and garage. When serving the search warrant, the suspect was not at home. We knew that the Sex Crimes detectives would arrest him in the following days. We did obtain two large boxes of evidence, which included both pornography and a large number of sex items.

While we were in Reporting, filing the Evidence Report, Steve reached in one of the boxes and pulled out a huge, 18 inch long, thick, flesh-colored dildo. As one can imagine, the wisecracks started flying around like wasps from an agitated hornet's nest. Steve held it up and said, "Wow, look at this!"

I responded, "Yeah, it reminds me a lot of myself."

Steve then held it next to my head and looked back and forth between my face and the dildo and said, "You're right. The resemblance is uncanny." After a few more exchanges regarding our alleged nicknames as the "anaconda of love," "the python of passion," or "boa constrictor of the boudoir," Steve finally asked, "Seriously, what should I do with this?"

Avoiding the obvious answer, I became the professional police officer. "It's just another piece of evidence. "Put your initials and Photo Number (badge number) on it and list it on the Evidence Report," I chuckled.

I went back to listing the evidence in my box and a few minutes later, Steve said, "How's this?" He had printed my name, R. F. Williams, and my Photo Number with Liquid Paper in large letters along the length of the dildo. I grabbed it from him and attempted to wipe my name and number off of the phallus, but only succeeded in smearing it.

I told Steve, "Well, this has obviously lost its evidential value." We hid it in the locker room for later use in a practical joke we had yet to conjure up. Later that month, we had an inspection. When the sergeant called us to attention, I had about 8 inches of the dildo hanging out of my right pant leg. Two lieutenants were conducting the inspection, Otto and Jerry. Otto came by first. He started at my head and looked down to my feet, but to my consternation, he didn't notice my "little friend" hanging out my pant leg. Lieutenant Jerry followed close behind and started out the same as Otto. When he got to my shoes, however, he did a double take and looked me in the face with wide eyes.

I looked down and then back at Lieutenant Jerry and deadpanned, "He's just showing off, Lieutenant. I'll play with him later and he'll be okay." Lieutenant Jerry was notorious for his lack of a sense of humor. In this case, however, he just grinned and moved on to inspect Steve.

15: You're Really Good Looking

I worked with Steve for a couple of years. He was a very good looking guy. I didn't really notice it until one night when we had to take a 5150 (psycho) to Harbor General for evaluation. On the way back to Long Beach, we stopped by my house in Rancho Palos Verdes. My wife and my mother-in-law, who lived with us, were home. The next day, my wife asked me about my partner, Steve. She told me that after we left, her mother had turned to her and said, "Now that was a good-looking man." This comment was out of character for her to make. Judi advised me that Steve was a very good looking guy.

One night, Steve and I were working up in North Long Beach. A couple of our officers were working as bouncers at a cowboy bar in that area called "The Silver Bullet." Between calls, I drove up to the front of the bar to talk to our two off-duty cops. Steve, on the passenger side, asked them how things were going. One of them said, "Great. You guys are just in time. It's Chippendale night and this place is packed with horny, half drunk women, and intermission just started."

Shortly after our bouncer friend made the statement, the crowd of raucous, tipsy young women started pouring out the front door. A couple of them approached Steve's passenger window. One of them looked at Steve and said, "Wow, you're really good looking." She stuck her head completely in the window, looked me right in the eye, then looked back at Steve and said, "Yeah, you're really good looking." Steve just looked at me with a shit-eating grin on his face. I hit the gas pedal and took off, with the girl spinning around after I almost took her head off before she could get it out of the window!

16: Passwords

While I was working with Steve, the department started putting computers in our cars. The Long Beach Police Department referred to our computers as KDTs. I can't remember what the initials stood for, if I ever knew. The Communications Division assigned us each a password. At a Squad Meeting one day the sergeant handed out envelopes from Communications that contained our individual passwords. Mine, I still remember, was "hill."

Now as good looking as Steve was, not every woman was enamored with him. Apparently, one or two of the dispatchers in Communications didn't particularly like Steve. When he got into our patrol car that night, he was cussing and grousing about the "witches" in Communications. Or at least he was using a word that rhymed with witches. When I asked him what was wrong, he told me that some of the ornery dispatchers didn't like him and assigned him a derogatory password. When I asked him what it was, he showed me the paper from Communications with the blank for his password filled in with the word "limp." Steve was a little sensitive about his password. He didn't laugh or even answer me when I asked if the dispatchers knew this from personal experience or just reputation.

17: Junior Sergeant Passover

Chris and I were in the Police Academy together. Years later, I finished one ahead of Chris on the sergeant's test. After making the first 16 people on the list sergeants, the Chief decided to give an additional non-civil service oral exam to the next three members on the list, I was number three. This was a low stress oral that lasted about half an hour. The Department then made sergeants of the next two members on the list. The Chief again decided to give an additional non-civil service oral to the next three officers on the list. This was a high stress oral that lasted an hour and a half.

About a week after this oral, I received a note to report to the Chief of Police's office.

When I got to the Chief's office, he invited me in and started the conversation by saying, "Have a seat, Officer

Williams." He addressed me as "Officer Williams." This is what we in police work call a clue.

The Chief continued, "I have some bad news for you. I am not making you sergeant at this time. It's not that you are not qualified. You are qualified. As a matter of fact, you are highly qualified. You're just not the most qualified." I was stunned, so stunned that I don't even remember him dismissing me. Chris called me the next day and told me that the Chief was promoting him to sergeant that Friday. He expressed his condolences and told me he didn't know what else he could do but accept the promotion.

I agreed and that was where we left it for the time being.

It took about five months, but I was finally promoted to sergeant, retroactive to one month after Chris. Could Chris, the little weasel, let sleeping dogs lie? Noooooo. He started referring to me as "Junior Sergeant." To this day, when I call his cell phone, his screen lights up with the words "Junior Sergeant."

A couple of years later, Chris was the sergeant in Forgery/Fraud and I was the sergeant in Gang Detectives. Chris's secretary, Debby, had a copy machine, and she had the expertise to make business cards. I brought her the stock blank business cards with the city and Police Department logo on them and she said she would make me a hundred cards. A day or so later, I picked them up. The cards looked great. At an annual Gang Investigators conference in Anaheim, I passed out a few cards. After giving one of my cards to an investigator from another city, he looked at the card and asked me, "What's a 'Junior Sergeant'?" I looked at the card and saw that was exactly what was printed under my name. That rat bastard Chris and his diabolical secretary had printed about half of my cards with the fake Junior Sergeant rank, and had buried them in the box of cards she gave me!

18: Avoiding Profanity

Sometime during my time as a street police officer, the higher ups decided that it was inappropriate to use profanity in any situation. We all understood that in most interactions with civilians it would not be proper to use "street" language. However, there are definitely times in high stress incidents when profanity can be used to dramatic effect, like exclamation points. For instance, when confronting an armed robber, it is much more effective to yell, "Drop that gun, asshole, or I'll fill you so full of lead you could use your pecker for a pencil!" than to shout, "Sir, please place your pistol on the ground or I will be forced to use my service weapon in a possibly deadly manner!"

Word came from on high that Internal Affairs (I.A.) cases were going to be opened whenever an officer used profanity, regardless of the circumstances. Instead of openly rebelling, I saw this as an opportunity to increase our collective vocabulary. I read a lot of books, and when I came upon an interesting word, I would memorize it and use it in my reports or when clearing calls on the radio. Sometimes I would clear a disturbance of the peace call by radioing in, "We advised and sent the miscreants on their way." When we made an arrest we might clear the call on the radio, "We have the malefactor in custody."

I had partnered a few times with an officer named Rory. He made me laugh when we stopped someone on the street because he would approach them and address them by saying, "Citizen, please show me your identification because you just violated our traffic code section against jaywalking." I decided that in addition to using alternative words and phrases for otherwise profane words, I would incorporate Rory's use of "citizen" when speaking to the people with whom we came in contact.

Some of my partners and I developed a list of words and phrases that even Internal Affairs could not find objectionable. After using these over a period of time, we found the added benefit was that many of the miscreants and malefactors we came in contact with became confused, befuddled and/or exasperated when speaking to us. This sometimes defused a tense situation.

After some trial and error, one of my partners pointed out that we could avoid a sustained I.A. complaint if we didn't directly call anyone a name. Instead, it was decided that we would say, "Sir, please stop acting like an asshole."

When we went for an interview in Internal Affairs, if they asked us if we "called the complainant an asshole," we could truthfully answer "no," because we had only said that he had been acting like whatever derogatory word we had used.

We also came up with non-obscene words for the most common English profanities. We started with the most overused obscenities. For motherfucker, we used the term maternal fornicator. Shithead became fecal cranium. Flaming asshole turned into incendiary rectum. Dirty cocksucker morphed into an unhygienic fellator. A rotten prick changed to a diseased appendage. A rat bastard was modified to an illegitimate rodent. A dumb ass was a mute equine. The words and phrases were only limited by our imaginations.

We would occasionally get feedback from our sergeant or officers in another unit. Once, after we told an obnoxious drunk that he was "acting like a diseased appendage," he later told the Booking Desk Sergeant that we had told him he had a "sick appendix." Often, the response to some of these phrases was, "Say what?" or "What do you mean?" The confusion this sometime caused in suspects allowed us to make arrests with a minimum use of force.

Part 6: The Booking Desk

1: Extortion at the Booking Desk

After making sergeant, I spent about a year on the night shift as the Booking Desk Sergeant. The Booking Desk is an "inside" job. It is where the officers bring their arrestees to be booked into the system. Other than the Booking Desk Sergeant, only clerk typists and stenos work there, typing in the information from the handwritten form given them by the arresting officers. Most of these stenos and clerk typists are female. (All of the other people working at the Booking Desk when I was there were female.) They are a hardworking crew, doing a thankless but very necessary job.

Interestingly enough, it was a very rare occasion when anyone ever gave the Booking Desk crew a hard time. This was because the booking of a prisoner could take from about 10 minutes to upwards of an hour and a half, depending on the mood of the steno or clerk, and how many prisoners there were to be booked at a given time. This story is illustrative: Patty was the senior employee in Booking on my shift.

One day, I came in with two boxes of chocolate bars that my two sons were required to sell for their Little League fund raising. I set them on the Booking Desk with a sign the read "$1." After the first hour of the shift, I had sold one chocolate bar. Patty asked me if I wanted her to sell the candy.

I said, "Sure, but how are you going to do better?"

She said, "Watch."

We had several officers at the Booking Desk at that time, and two of our clerks were to file the booking sheets. One of the officers came up and handed Patty his handwritten sheet. Patty asked him if he wanted to buy a candy bar and the officer declined. Another officer was just finishing up his booking sheet, so Patty motioned him over and asked him if he would like to buy a candy bar. He immediately responded with, "Yes, I would," and pulled out a dollar bill and handed it to Patty. She asked if he was done with his sheet, which he had just completed. Patty took his sheet and left the first officer standing there waiting. That night I sold out both boxes. I was happy, having done my duty to help my boys fund their Little League. However, a day or so later, my sons came home with two more boxes of chocolate bars. Their coach was so happy that two of his team members had sold their boxes on the first day that he gave them each another box to sell. I told Patty and the other girls to slow down a little on their strongarm tactics!

2: Clowns at the Booking Desk

The good thing about the afternoon shift in Booking was that you were able to see officers on all three shifts. LBPD Patrol worked a 10/40 work schedule, which meant the officers worked 10 hour days, four days a week. The day shift's official end of watch time off was 5:30 PM. Afternoons started at 4:30 PM and the graveyard shift started at 10:30 PM. The afternoon booking sergeant's shift began at 4PM and ended at midnight, so it overlapped all the shifts.

One of the day shift officers who came in quite often was Terry. Terry was a big, muscular guy with a goofy sense of humor. Terry would usually play mind games with his prisoners while filing out the booking sheets. In the upper right hand corner of the booking sheet was a box that contained four or five health questions. This was before anyone had heard of AIDS, so the questions were something like: Do you have an open wound? Do you use heroin? Do you have a sexually transmitted disease? Do you have hepatitis? Have you ever had TB?

Terry would ask his prisoner all of those questions and then, after the TB question, he would ask, "Do you watch color TV?"

The prisoner would invariably come back with words to the effect, "Yeah, I watch color TV. What's wrong with that?" Terry then went into his frightening rant about how the gamma rays from color TV would at first cause infertility in men and ultimately cause impotence.

"Man, if you want kids, don't watch color television. If you want to get a hard-on after age 30 (or 40 or 50, depending on the age of his prisoner), don't get near a color TV." I know there are still a few of Terry's prisoners who won't go near a color TV!

The last question Terry would ask, after scaring the hell out of the prisoner about gamma rays, was, "Are you oozing?" Only Terry wouldn't just say oozing, he drew out the o's so that it was ooooooooozing. I think Terry just liked the sound of the word, but when the prisoner asked what oozing was, Terry would go into another convoluted story that was calculated to confuse and horrify the prisoner!

3: King of Sexual Harassment

After working at the Booking Desk for a couple months, Christmas rolled around. I don't remember what I got the women on my shift for Christmas that year, but they chipped in and bought me a personalized coffee cup. It was beautiful. On one side, it was emblazoned with the Long Beach Police badge, with my name, rank, and badge number. On the other side, in all capital letters, was the phrase, "THE KING OF SEXUAL HARASSMENT." They all laughed uproariously when they saw my face when I read the phrase. It was a running joke in Booking. Almost any comment, joke, or statement out of a male's mouth, one of the steno's, usually Patti or Lori, would say, "That's sexual harassment." If I was the target of their mocking sexual harassment claim, I would indignantly yell back words to the effect, "Harassment, harassment,

I never touched her assment. I may have looked at her boobments, but she wanted me to." So that cup brought smiles to all our faces. I loved that cup. Unfortunately, a couple of years after I transferred out of Booking, I dropped the cup and broke it.

Shortly after Christmas, one of the stenos had a birthday. I went to the mug shop that was on Redondo and bought the steno a coffee mug. It was similar to mine. It had the badge and her name on one side. On the other side was printed the phrase, "I'M PROUD TO BE ONE OF BUZ'S BITCHES."

When their birthdays came around, each of the women on my shift let me know they wanted one of those mugs. Soon, every steno on my shift soon had one. The stenos from the other shifts began requesting the mugs for their birthdays.

One busy night, Elaine had come to Booking to help us. I asked Elaine if she could run one of the prisoners for warrants. Elaine said "No" and went back to whatever paperwork she was doing.

I asked, "Elaine, why not?"

Elaine looked up and said, "Because I'm not one of your bitches."

I laughed and told her to "Stand up and raise your right hand. Repeat after me: I will be nobody's bitch but Buz's Bitch from now on and hence forward." Elaine received her mug the following week!

The last mug I gave was about four years later. After working the Booking Desk for a year, I requested a transfer to the Vice Section. The lieutenant, Dick, and I had become friends working on a committee seeking to change the Booking form and he advised me to put in for the job. After I conducted a Squad Meeting one day, one of the female officers, Merit, approached me saying, "Sarge, I want to be one of your Bitches."

Merit later transferred to another department. When she first used the cup at her new department, some of the officers would see it and give her some rather quizzical looks. I saw Merit after I retired and she told me that she was still working at that other department and still had her cup.

We worked hard in Booking, but we also had a lot of fun. In today's politically correct atmosphere, where people are afraid to laugh or say anything, I wonder if men and women can work together with anywhere near the congeniality that we did.

Part 7: Miscellaneous Comics

1: Previous Vice Cop Frolics

There were two guys in Vice in the 1970s and '80s who reached iconic stature in the Long Beach Police Department. Richard and David were both big, strong men. Both were affable, funny, and tough. I first met Richard on December 31, 1974. At that time, officers were required to qualify with their duty weapon every month. One month, Richard and I were apparently the only officers in the Department who hadn't qualified.

It was raining. Richard and I were waiting for the weather to let up a little so we could shoot. (Please note that the first year an officer works, he or she is considered a rookie.) Richard introduced himself to me, inquired as to my rookie status, and asked me where I worked. Then, he started telling me his latest war story.

The night before, at about dusk, he and David had gone into the men's room on the beach at the foot of

Granada. (It should be noted that a subset of the male homosexual community derives sexual excitement from engaging in sexual acts in public places and the danger of getting arrested while occupied in these acts.)

Upon entering the public restroom they viewed a carnival of sexual activity. Richard said that he and David were hugging each other and whispering into each other's ears. "In stall one, the bald guy in the red sweater is getting a blow job from a guy in a striped shirt. In stall two, the big fat guy is sodomizing the skinny black guy," etc. etc. When they figured they had identified everyone in the restroom and what they were doing, David walked out to their car in the parking lot and called for the Paddy Wagon to assist them in making arrests. Then David walked back into the restroom and they waited for the assistance.

A short time later, the Wagon arrived and Officer Paul and his rookie walked into the men's room. The rookie's eyes opened to the size of saucers when he saw what was going on. David saw this and grabbed his shoulder. Before David could say anything, the rookie pulled out his nightstick and drew it back to strike whoever he thought was trying to make him the object of his affection. In the darkening defecatorium, Richard and David convinced him they were Vice Officers before any "stick time" occurred.

Richard said that he stood at the door of the restroom as David escorted each of the lewd conduct violators out. Richard would cuff the individuals and then hand them off to Paul and his partner who placed them in the van.

The last guy out was a loud, antagonistic, skinny dude. As Richard was handcuffing him, the guy told Richard words to the affect that if Richard was so tough, he should take the handcuffs off, go out on the sand, and the prisoner would "kick the shit" out of Richard. Not one easily intimidated, Richard uncuffed the suspect, grabbed him by the collar and walked him to the sand behind the men's room. Richard let go of the prisoner and said, "Okay, go ahead."

The prisoner then retorted, "You first."

So Richard hit the guy in the head and he went down to his knees. Richard grabbed him, and the prisoner said, "I give up. You win."

Richard told the fella, "Oh, no. You put the dime in the jukebox, you're gonna hear the whole song." Richard then slapped the guy up the side of the head, handcuffed him, and put him in the Paddy Wagon.

At the station, David and Richard parked their car while Paul and his partner started pulling the prisoners out of the wagon. They all came out peacefully except the same fella that had wanted to fight Richard. He was yelling at Paul as Richard came around the vehicle and looked in. The prisoner saw Richard and immediately stopped his ranting. "I'll come peaceful, Mister Richard. I don't want you to play the flip side of that record!"

2: David and the Bull

You may not believe this story, but few who knew David doubt it didn't happen. After I had been on the Department a year or so, my wife, Judi, and I and another couple with whom she worked went to Ensenada, Mexico for a few days. On our first night, the four of us were walking one of the streets, where most of the nightclubs were in full swing. Through one of the open windows in one of the nightclubs, I heard someone yelling, "Hey, Long Beach." I looked up and saw Richard. He said, "Why don't you guys come in and I'll buy you some drinks?" How could we refuse?

It was standing room only in the bar, but Richard dragged us all over to a table by the window. He introduced us to his partner, David, and another Long Beach cop named Cy, all of whom worked in the Vice Squad.

Richard insisted on paying for our cocktails. He said they had to drive down from Tijuana because they couldn't go anywhere in that town without getting "shitfaced drunk." Everyone there recognized David and would buy them drinks!

Richard continued, "Yesterday, we went to the Bull Fights in TJ. One of the matadors didn't know what he was doing. The crowd was booing and throwing things into the ring. All of a sudden, David, who is half in the bag, and Jim, another big Vice officer, jump into the ring. David runs up to the bull, grabs it around the neck in the standard police restraining hold, and chokes the bull out while Jim attempts to 'belly bomp' the bull. David lets go and the bull drops to the ground unconscious. The crowd exploded. David took a couple of bows, walked over, and got back into the stands. Every bar and restaurant we went into, the customers recognized David and bought us drinks. We had to get out of Tijuana or we would all have died of alcohol poisoning."

3: Chatty Cathy

Richard had joined the Long Beach Police Department after serving in the Marine Corp in Viet Nam. He followed in the footsteps of his older brother, John, who was every bit as witty and funny as Richard. In late 1989, both John and Richard had been elected to the police union's Board of Directors of the Long Beach Police Officers Association (LBPOA). I had been elected to that organization, too. At that time, the LBPOA held an annual dinner to install newly elected board members and executive officers, and to honor those officers who had retired the year before. They called it the Installation and Retirement Dinner. (A few years later, the LBPOA added an officer of the year ceremony, a Richard A. Rose Career Achievement Award ceremony, and a Mike Sergei Award ceremony. However, in 1989, the LBPOA just had this annual celebration.)

While at my first Installation and retirement party, held at the Petroleum Club, Judi and I were seated between John and Richard. One of the speakers at the dinner told a funny story or joke, and after the laughter had died down, Richard looked across Judi and me and said to his brother, John, "That's sounds like the Chatty Cathy thing that happened at Christmas." John and Richard began laughing uproariously. Judi and I couldn't help but laugh along with the two brothers, infected by their joviality.

After some prodding, John and Richard agreed to tell us the Chatty Cathy story. Every Christmas Day, one of the brothers hosted the Christmas dinner and the other brought over a bottle of Crown Royal. While their wives cooked the turkey and side dishes, John and Richard would discuss various subjects, such as sports and family affairs, and watch football on TV. They would also consume the contents of the Crown Royal bottle.

On this particular Christmas day, more than a decade before, John was hosting the feast, so Richard brought the Crown Royal. Before he could uncork the adult nectar, Judy, one of John's daughters, had a doll in her hand and came running over saying, "Uncle Richard, Uncle Richard, look at my Chatty Cathy doll." As she said this, Judy was pulling on a string on the side of the doll's neck. She stopped in front of her uncle and again pulled the string. In Judy's voice, the doll repeated, "Uncle Richard, Uncle Richard, look at my Chatty Cathy doll." At this point, Judy saw her cousin, Chris, and sat the doll down on the coffee table in front of Richard and ran off to play with Chris.

It should be noted that, at this time Richard was working Vice. When one is working Vice, he comes into daily contact with pimps, prostitutes, johns, and homosexuals having sex in public places, usually men's rooms. Some people think that Vice cops develop a jaundiced attitude toward anything sexual. Vice cops would argue that they just find the humor in all human sexual encounters.

At any rate, Richard picked up little Chatty Cathy, pulled her string and said, "Fuck me, fuck me, stick it up my ass. Make me write bad checks," or words in a similarly profane vain. Richard then pulled the string and Chatty repeated the obscene statement in Richard's voice, causing John and Richard to collapse into fits of laughter. The brothers than began a serious attack on the Crown Royal.

An hour or so later, with the Crown Royal bottle almost empty, John's in-laws arrived, fresh from their Christmas church services. When little Judy saw her grandparents, she ran to them, grabbing her Chatty Cathy doll off the coffee table as she went. She started yelling, "Grandma, Grandpa, look at my Chatty Cathy doll" as she pulled the string. As often happens in such situations, all conversations and background noise ceased, as Chatty Cathy spewed out, "Fuck me, fuck me, stick it up my ass. Make me write bad checks," all in Richard's very recognizable voice. Judy stopped in her tracks and all eyes turned to Richard, who was attempting to crawl out of the room, as Judy said, "Uncle Richard, how could you?"

4: Testifying on a Lewd Conduct Case

Richard and Dave once arrested a man in a public restroom for masturbating in public. Richard was subpoenaed to court to testify. After being sworn in, Richard testified that he saw the defendant stroking his erect penis while standing at the urinal. On cross examination, the defendant's attorney asked Richard, "Was the defendant's penis in a flaccid state when you first saw him?"

Richard paused a minute, smiled, looked at the jury and responded, "No, sir, it was right here in California." The jury laughed. The prosecutor laughed. The defendant and his attorney laughed.

The judge, who was not laughing, banged his gavel once, leaned over toward the witness box, and said, "That will be enough of that, Detective."

5: Richard at the Police Picnic

Once a year, the Long Beach Police Officers Association puts on a picnic at their picnic grounds adjacent to the Police Firing Range. One year, when our two sons were about 3 and 1, Judi and I took them with us. Our oldest son, Richie, was off playing one of the games that Sergeant Todd presided over for small children. Our youngest, Matt, whom I nicknamed "Moose" because he was such a big baby, was standing next to his mother on our picnic blanket.

Richard, who had a day off from Vice, was walking by and greeted me. He then saw Moose, who was still pretty stocky at a little less than a year old. Richard bent down, picked up Moose and asked, "Who's this big boy?" Moose proceeded to ball his fist and hit Richard in the nose.

Richard just laughed and said, "I like this kid!"

Judi looked at me and said, "Tell him to give me back my baby."

I glanced at Richard, who was six foot three inches and 250 pounds of pure muscle, and told her, "You tell him to give you back your baby!"

Part 8: Adventures in Vice

How I Got to Vice

On the Long Beach Police Department, when an officer is promoted to sergeant, he or she is placed in one of the less desirable positions. This is usually an "inside" job, such as the Communications Sergeant, Jail Sergeant or the Booking Sergeant. The new sergeant usually stays in that job until a new rash of promotions allows him to transfer to a more preferred sergeant's job. I was first assigned to the Booking Desk. While I was still working the Booking Desk, I noticed that a lot of crooks who were on probation or parole were being released on their own recognizance or on bail. (If a parolee or probationer is arrested, their Probation Officer or Parole Agent could put a hold on them that would keep them in custody at least until their first court appearance. However, we were letting a lot of these professional criminals out because there was nothing on the Booking Form that asked if they were so legally encumbered.)

I wrote up a change in the booking procedure that prevented this from reoccurring and sent it to the Chief of Police. He liked the idea and formed a committee to study the change. I was put on the committee with the Jail Commander and the Vice Lieutenant, Dick. Dick and I got along really well.

As I was nearing the end of my term as a Booking Sergeant, Dick told me to put in for the Vice Sergeant's position, which I did. Normally, the Booking Sergeant would return to Patrol for a couple years before going to Detectives, if he so chose. While Patrol is where the action is, detectives make more money and usually work business hours. The exception is the Special Investigation Division of the Detective Bureau, which includes Vice and Narcotics. The detectives in those units work all kinds of hours because the objects or their investigations are engaged in their illegal activities (dope dealing, prostitution, illegal gambling, etc.) at all hours of the day or night. The Chief of Police has to approve anyone who gets assigned to those units because if a police department is susceptible to corruption, it usually starts in those units, because most people, including a lot of cops, believe those are victimless crimes.

At any rate, I passed the Chief's approval and, fortunately, got the Vice assignment. I started working there in the summer of 1986.

Section 1: Cases

1: The Stutterer

The street Vice Sergeant's job was a working position, which meant that you made work schedules and planned special John Programs, Lewd Conduct Programs, Bar Complaints, etc. You also worked as the bait and back-up for arresting prostitutes and lewd conduct violators in the many city men's rooms. When I started working Vice, the state law was that the vice officer in a prostitution contact could mention either the sex act or the money, but not both. Our department policy was that the vice officer could not mention either the sex act or the money.

One of my first days in Vice, I was told that I was going to be the "bait" for a prostitution run. I was given the keys to one of our "Ugly Duck" rentals and told to go up on Pacific Coast Highway and arrest hookers. I knew that I couldn't mention the sex or the money, so I was trying to think of a way to get the working girls to solicit without my mentioning either.

I saw a street hooker on the southwest corner of PCH and Daisy Avenue and pulled over. I already had my passenger side window open, and the girl approached and said, "Are you looking for a date?"

I told her, "Yyyyyes."

She responded with, "Are you a cop?"

I shook my head and said, "Na, na, na, na, no."

She opened the door and sat in the passenger seat. She turned to me and said, "What do you want?" I looked right at her and said, "I d-d-d-don't know. I, I, I'm n-n-new at this. Wha, wha what do you suggest?"

She said, "The way it works is you gotta tell me what you want."

I told her, "Oh, oh, okay. How about a b-b-b-b-b-b-b-b-b..." Before I could blurt out any more b's, she interrupted and asked, "blow job?"

I nodded.

"What do you want to pay for that?" she inquired

"Ta, ta, ta, ta, ta,." and before I could continue she said, "Twenty?"

"N-n-no," I said, "T-t-ten."

"I won't blow you for ten, it'll cost you twenty. Okay?"

I nodded my assent, pulled from the curb and gave my back-up the prearranged signal. When I saw them get behind me, I pulled over and they came running up and arrested her. I had popped my first whore! Er, um, that is, I had arrested my first prostitute.

2: The Deaf John

The use of stuttering to get the prostitutes to make both the money and sex act propositions worked pretty well for a couple of months, but the street hookers were starting to catch on. So I came up with an alternative that worked even better: The Deaf Guy. The first time I tried it, it worked like a charm. I pulled over on PCH near Magnolia after passing a girl about fifty yards behind me. She came running up to the open passenger window, stuck her head in, and asked, "Are you looking to party?"

In the best imitation of a deaf man I knew, I responded in a nasally voice, "Yeth, I am. Bah I'm deaf an I onny weed lips, so your gonna hafta talk kinna slow."

Moving her mouth in a slow, deliberate, exaggerated manner, the girl said. "Oh, I-under-stand-completely. Can-I-get-in-your-car?"

"Oh, shure. Op white on in."

After she was seated in the undercover car, she would tap me on my right arm so that I would look at her before she said anything. The first time she asked, "What-do-you-want?"

I told her, "Gee, I'm kinna new at this. What do you suggest?"

She tapped me on my right arm again and stated, "How-about-half-and-half?"

I looked at her quizzically and inquired, "What?"

After the preliminary arm tap, she looked at me and made a motion with her closed right fist toward her mouth, which I took to mean the performance of oral copulation. She then made a circle with her left thumb and forefinger and proceeded to penetrate the circle with her right index finger. I took this to mean normal sexual intercourse. Actually, I was already familiar that the term "half and half," as it was the street name for doing those two acts.

I smiled at her and said, "Oh, that would be just swell!"

She smiled back at me, held up three fingers on her left hand and told me, "That-costs-thirty-dollars."

I widened my eyes while looking at her and asked, "Three dollars?"

The girl shook her head, waved her hands and said, "No-no. Thirty-dollars." While she was saying this, she again held up three fingers on her left hand and, next to it, she made a circle with her right hand so that I would understand the full price for her services. When I nodded my head in agreement to her price, she pointed ahead on the street and then gave me a pat on the arm. When I looked back at her, she told me to "turn right at the light." After that turn, she tapped me again and she said, "Turn left at the For Sale sign."

I made the turn and stopped in front of the house with the For Sale sign, having already given the prearranged signal to my back-up team. When I put the car in park, the hooker hit me a little more ardently on my arm. "Why-did-you-stop?"

"You told me to stop at the For Sale sign," I responded.

A little more frantically, she stated, "No. I-told-you-to-turn-at-the-For-Sale-sign."

"Then why did you tell me to stop?" I inquired.

Panicky now, she told me, "I didn't tell you to stop."

By this time, my back-up undercover vice cops, Rob and Pat, were at her door. Pat opened the door and, showing his badge and ID, said, "Long Beach Vice. You're under arrest for soliciting for prostitution."

Not ready to surrender yet, the hooker looked at the two vice cops and said, "But this is just my deaf friend who's taking me home."

In my best deaf voice, I said, "Yeth, that's right, what seems to be the problem, offither?"

Rob looked at me through the open door and told me, "Shut up, you deaf motherfucker!"

With those words the working girl became protective and a little combative, saying, "Don't call him that." With some effort, Pat and Rob handcuffed her and placed her in the backseat of their car after making sure that she didn't have any weapons. They followed me back to PCH, where I was able to get three other street hookers to fall for the deaf guy routine. Pat and Rob told me later that, after the second arrest, the first girl told them, "He's not deaf. He's a cop." No one ever said you had to be a genius to be a "working girl."

3: Jim and the Van

Most of the prostitutes were on Pacific Coast Highway between the west city limits and Junipero. Occasionally, the situation would occur when some of the Vice officers had training or there was a combination of officers who had called in sick, or when other guys had vacations or holidays, and there weren't enough officers to do the usual prostitute run on the highway. It didn't happen very often, but it did happen.

On one of those occasions, Jim and I were the only ones available to go out in the streets. With just two officers, we really couldn't take two cars because the back-up officer had to be close in proximity when the arrest of the prostitute took place. We had, for just such occasions, a plain, white, beat-up Ford van. It had two captain chairs in the front, a curtain behind those chairs, two captain chairs toward the rear of the van, and two big bean bag chairs. The back-up officer would get behind the rear captain chairs and cover himself with the bean bag chairs.

On this particular day, I was the bait cop and Jim sat in on one of the rear captain chairs, with the curtain mostly closed. As I was driving west on PCH, there was a prostitute sitting on the bus bench in front of Long Beach City College. I told Jim and, as I was pulling over, he jumped behind one of the rear captain chairs and covered himself with the two bean bag chairs. The hooker came running up, and without even asking, opened the passenger side door and got in. I went through my "deaf guy" routine and she agreed to screw me for twenty dollars. She then directed me to drive two blocks, turn right, and pull to the curb.

After I parked the van, I told her, in my "deaf guy" accent, that she should get ready in the back of the van and I would lock up the front. Once she got past the curtains, Jim jumped up with his badge and ID and placed her under arrest. We took her to the station and booked her. This was the first time Jim had actually heard my "deaf guy" act and was impressed.

Later, Jim went to some of the hearing aid businesses in Long Beach and obtained a broken hearing aid. (Nowadays, Jim actually uses a real hearing aid, although it is my opinion that he needs two!) The very next week, Jim and I were again the only two Vice cops available, and we took our van out again. This time Jim was the bait cop and I was in the back. The same prostitute we had arrested the week before was sitting on the same bus bench in front of Long Beach City College. I yelled to Jim that he shouldn't use the "deaf guy" ruse because it was the same gal we had arrested the week before. Because Jim had his new broken hearing aid in one of his ears, though, he didn't hear me.

It didn't matter. Jim did the same "deaf" act I had performed the week before. She solicited Jim for the same sex act for the same amount of money and directed him to the same location as the week before! When she came by the curtains, I showed her my badge and ID, told her she was under arrest and handcuffed her. I asked her, "Didn't I arrest you last week in this exact same van, at this exact same location, using the exact same 'deaf guy' trick on you? Couldn't you even catch the clue that we were Vice?"

She looked at me with her vacant doe eyes and said, "Well, at least I knew it wasn't the same deaf guy."

Jim and I both continued using the deaf guy prank on the hookers the rest of our time in Vice. I don't know for sure, but I don't think many deaf men were getting laid by hookers in Long Beach after that.

4: The John Priest

Jim was the consummate vice officer. The best vice cops are actors, ad libbers, and bullshit artists. Jim possessed all three qualities in abundance. One day, Jim came in with a priest's collar and shirt. He took on the persona of Father Mulcahy (from the movie and TV show M*A*S*H). We put him in a bait car and sent him out with a back-up team in a plain car. The first street prostitute Jim stopped for approached his car and asked if he was looking for a date. When she saw his Roman collar, she said, "Well, Father, I know you're a man and have needs like any other man. What kind of fun are you looking for today?" Father Mulcahy arrested four or five girls that day. Only one girl looked at Jim, and believing he was a priest, shook her head and said, "No way!"

5: Tow Truck Driver

Jim took it upon himself to borrow one of the city tow trucks to pick up hookers one night. It worked out great. Every time Jim stopped for one of the "ladies of the evening," the girl would come running up to the tow truck. They would each make a similar statement. In so many words, they would each say something like, "Oh, I thought I knew all of the tow truck drivers. You must be new." We made half a dozen arrests using the city tow truck that night. The only downside was that the city refused to let us use their tow trucks after that night. I wonder why!

6: New Lieutenant Gets a Leg Up in Vice

A year or so into my time in Vice, our lieutenant, Dick, transferred out. Our new lieutenant was Mike, who had been a past President of the Police Officers Association. I knew Mike, liked him, and was sure we would work well together. During Mike's first week in Vice, we had a prostitution program. We parked our van over on San Francisco Street, which was in an out of the way industrial area, and used it as a booking van. Then we would send out our "bait" and back-up cars, and arrest as many hookers as possible. We brought them back to the booking van, filled out the booking sheets, and when we had a full van we transported them to the booking desk.

On one occasion, we rented a big rig, minus the trailer, and put Rich as the bait officer driving it. Lieutenant Mike was riding with me, and I was showing him how we arrested these soiled doves who plied their wares on public streets.

We saw Rich pull over and stop on PCH and Magnolia and pick up a black prostitute I recognized. This particular girl had a prosthetic leg, and every time we arrested her she would fight. (After one of her arrests by Pat and Rob, she was put in the back of their undercover back-up car fighting the whole way. Pat got into the backseat with her and Rob was about to drive to the station when he realized he had left his handheld radio on the roof of the car. With the engine running, Rob jumped out of the car to grab the radio. As he did so, the prostitute kicked the car into gear and it started crossing Pacific Coast Highway during rush hour traffic. Thankfully, Rob was able to chase the car on PCH and get in and stop it before it struck another vehicle or a light standard.) I told the lieutenant about this hooker fighting every time she got arrested. For whatever reason, I failed to mention that she had a fake leg. We weren't Rich's primary back-up, but because the girl always fought, the lieutenant and I decided to assist and started following the semi. Rich drove the semi east on PCH, then started going northbound on Cherry, and then into the oil fields of Signal Hill. Rich was an extremely good Vice cop. He didn't look like a cop and usually got a solicitation from a hooker within a block or two of picking one up. So this was an extraordinarily long time for Rich to have a hooker in his vehicle without giving the hit signal. Finally, in the oil field, Rich gave the sign and pulled over next to an oil derrick. Even before the semi came to a complete stop, the passenger door opened, and the prostitute jumped out. Unfortunately for her she landed on her prosthetic leg and instantly fell to ground and began thrashing. Lieutenant Mike and I were the closest to the semi and the first to reach her. Her phony leg was still in her pant leg but it was bent 180 degrees opposite of the way a leg is supposed to bend. Mike, in his Southern accent, looked at the hooker's very injured leg and blurted out, "Oh, Lord!"

The two back-up Vice officers, Ted and Bill, came running up just then. Bill grabbed the foot of the prosthetic leg and flung it away from the thrashing working girl, saying, "Don't worry about a lawsuit Lieutenant, she doesn't have a leg to stand on now!"

7: Clogging at Floyd's

When the classic steak, prime rib, and lobster restaurant, Valentines, on Anaheim Street in East Long Beach closed down, it was renovated into a gay cowboy bar called Floyd's. It was a pretty high class bar and we were a little surprised when a complaint from there was phoned in. Detectives Bob and Jim were sent to check the veracity of the complaint. When they arrived, there was a group of men in denims, suspenders, and cowboy boots who were learning how to clog dance.

Bob and Jim walked past the cloggers, sat at the bar and ordered bottled beer. They watched the lesson as they drank their beers. The lesson ended before they finished their beers and as the cloggers were packing up their gym bags, someone had put a coin in the jukebox and a slow country and western love song started playing. By this time, Jim and Bob had turned around to face the bar. Jim felt a tap on his shoulder and turned to see a man smiling at him. Jim returned the smile and the man asked Jim if he would like to dance.

Being a happily married heterosexual with four sons, Jim was a little taken aback by the request, but recovered quickly. He motioned with his hand to Bob and said, "Oh, I'm sorry, I'm with him."

Bob, never being one to pass up an occasion to rat-fuck a coworker, smiled and said, "Oh, I don't mind. Go ahead and dance with him."

Jim demurred, stating, "I really don't feel like dancing right now," while turning back to Bob and giving him the stink eye.

8: "Oh, Listen to Me, I'm Such a Tramp"

One of the most difficult things to learn in the Vice Squad was how to talk to the different people you encountered when working the streets. For example, you wouldn't talk to a bookmaker the same way you'd talk to a prostitute. Similarly, heterosexual males working vice found it easier to talk to female prostitutes than to male hustlers or lewd conduct violators. Experience and hit or miss attempts would teach the novice Vice officer the proper nomenclature to use in a given situation.

Late one afternoon, we were working a complaint in one of the beach parking lots. Gay men used this parking lot as a cruising location. A man would park in his car and another man would walk by, make eye contact, and instead of renting a motel room or going to either's home or apartment they'd engage in a sexual act in the car, in public view in the parking lot. We would make arrests for lewd conduct or for soliciting for a lewd act.

On this particular day, we had two officers sitting in their undercover cars and four officers walking on the sidewalk next to the sand. Ted went to check to see if any lewd acts were going on in the public restroom located about fifty feet from the parking lot.

As I was walking along the sidewalk, a man in a sedan smiled at me and called out, “Hi, there.” I returned the smile, said hello, and walked toward the driver’s window of his car. Often, the men parked in the lot would be masturbating as they looked at other men on the beach or in the parking lot.

This man and I had just started our conversation when Ted came back into view after checking the restroom. When he saw Ted, this guy blurted out, “Look at that guy. He’s soooo cute. Oh, listen to me. I’m such a tramp.” Since it was obvious that he had the hots for Ted, I agreed that Ted was cute, ended the verbal contact and walked away.

Out of sight of this lust-crazed fellow, I signaled Ted. I gave him the info about the guy, his location, and car and went back to looking for other possible violations. Ted went and made contact with the man. It was obvious to Ted that the guy wasn’t going to break a law at that time, but he did arrange to meet Ted later to go dancing. Unfortunately, Ted stood him up!

A week later, Bill and I were working the other end of this same parking lot. I walked by a possible suspect who was sitting in a panel truck with gardening equipment in the back. He smiled and motioned to me. I came back to his car and stuck my head in the open passenger window. The man asked, "Why don't you get in the car and talk for a while? It's such a nice day." I did just that and we talked for some time. He steered the conversation to sexual and homosexual topics, but never attempted to touch me or suggest a lewd act in public, so we just talked.

Bill walked by once. After about ten minutes, he walked by again and gave me a look that said, "What's taking so long?" I was about ready to call it quits when I remembered the words from the week before. I pointed at Bill and said, "Look at that guy. He's soooo cute. Oh, listen to me. I'm such a tramp." The suspect then reached out and groped me. I gave Bill the signal and had one hand handcuffed before Bill even got to the car!

9: It's Not Yours

While I was a sergeant in Vice, the Department started a program that transferred rookie cops up to detectives for a few months. Some of these young officers worked two weeks in Narcotics and then two weeks in Vice. For a lot of these new rookies, Vice was a culture shock. Most of them could handle working bookmakers and it was good training in surveillance and following suspect vehicles. Although it was more difficult trying to pick up female prostitutes, most of the probationers would catch on. However, working lewd conduct violators proved to be a difficult hurdle for some of the more macho male rookies.

The regular Vice officers explained how a lewd conduct arrest would go down. In Long Beach, most of the lewd activity occurred in public men's rooms or, occasionally, in bushes in the city's parks or beaches. If you walked into a public men's room and you saw a man masturbating, that was an arrestable offense under the state's lewd conduct statute. If you saw a man orally copulating another man, they both could be arrested. If you observed a man sodomizing another man, both might be arrested. (Similarly, if you saw a man and a woman having sex in a car on a public street, they both may well be taken into custody for a violation of the lewd conduct law.)

To discourage two men going into the stalls together for sex, none of the toilet stalls had doors on them. Many of the lewd conduct violators would wait at the urinal or toilet with their penises out of their pants. They would stand this way for long periods after urinating, or without urinating at all. Sometimes the suspect would look over his shoulder, and if someone was looking at him he turned toward that person and started masturbating. Once in a while, when an undercover Vice officer walked into a men's room or had been standing there for some time, a violator came up and groped the cop's unexposed genitals, unsolicited, through his pants. This constituted a lewd conduct act and that guy was arrested.

This astounded some of our rookies. More than a few would make a statement to the affect that "anyone who grabs my dick is going to get flattened." As the sergeant, I would explain to these obstreperous young cops that striking a lewd conduct violator, who was not resisting arrest, was not acceptable and would lead to an Internal Affairs case, and possible suspension or worse. Many explained that they would feel "personally violated" if another man grabbed their "junk."

I had to explain to them that they shouldn't take it personally. They would come back at me and say, "If someone grabs your dick, how can you not take it personally?" I informed them, "When you work Vice, that is not your dick, it belongs to the city!"

10: Mike's Corral

Mike's Corral (which was later renamed the more graphic "Pistons") was a gay leather bar on Artesia Blvd in North Long Beach. It had both an inside bar and a fenced in patio area. We received a complaint that there were some lewd conduct incidents occurring in the patio area. Steve and I were working Vice at the time, so one night we decided to do a bar check at Mike's Corral.

Steve went in first, directly to the patio. I waited in the undercover car for a few minutes and then went into the bar and stayed in that area. The plan was that if there was a violation in the patio, Steve would come in and give me the prearranged signal and we'd either made an arrest or call for a patrol car to assist us. I would go to the patio and do the same if I saw a violation in the bar area. When I sat at the bar, the bartender approached and asked me what I would like.

Figuring a gay man who was going to a leather bar for the first time might order wine, I said that I would like a Chablis. When it came in a wine glass, I realized that I had violated one of the unwritten rules of undercover Vice cops when doing bar checks: "Don't order any beverage that is not served in a bottle."

The reason is that a lot of bars are less than hygienic in washing their glasses, not to mention the unwashed hands of some of the bartenders in the lower class bars. So, without taking so much as a sip from the glass, I wandered around the bar area for a few minutes. Then I went into the restroom to see if there was any funny stuff going on in there, and to dump the Chablis in the toilet when no one was looking. No one was in the john, so I poured out the Chablis. Back at the bar, I set the empty glass down and the bartender came over and asked if I wanted another Chablis. I told him that I thought I would like to switch to a Budweiser and he then asked, "Draft or bottle?" I said I would like a bottle, which he immediately opened and set in front of me.

I turned and looked around the bar. A minute or so later, Steve came in from the patio area. He looked around and then came over and sat at a table near my seat at the bar. Since he didn't give me a signal, I assumed that there had been no lewd conduct or ABC (Alcohol Beverage Control) violations on the patio. After a minute, I took my beer and sat at Steve's table. We quietly told each other that no one was doing anything illegal that night. We were about to leave when an obviously drunk man in his fifties came in and sat at the bar. He ordered a cocktail and the bartender made and served it to the drunk.

It is a violation of California state law to serve alcohol to an obviously intoxicated individual, so Steve left the bar to go call for a patrol unit to come and write the bartender a ticket and arrest the guy for being drunk in public. Unfortunately, when Steve radioed in, the dispatcher advised that there were no units available. We were going to have to blow our cover by writing the citation and making the arrest ourselves. Since we were on loan to nights because of vacations on the night shift, we didn't consider this a major impediment. We wrote the bartender his citation, then walked the drunk outside where we patted him down and arrested him.

While we were driving to the station, our prisoner kept asking what he was under arrest for and we continued to tell him that he was going to jail for being drunk in public. He informed us that he had gotten off work a few hours before. He worked about a mile and a half from Mike's Coral. He was walking home so he wouldn't drive drunk and was stopping at every bar along the way for a drink. He asked us, "If you can't be drunk in a bar, where can you be drunk?" A good question, but I told him that we may have saved him from being sexually molested.

He asked how that could be and I told him that Mike's was a gay leather bar and, as drunk as he was, he might have passed out after that last drink and several of the other customers might have taken advantage of him while he was out cold. He disputed the fact that Mike's

Corral was a gay bar, but when I asked him if he saw any women in there, and if he noticed that several of the men in Mike's were shirtless but wearing leather vests and nipple rings, his attitude changed. "Son of bitch, you're right. Thank you, guys, you saved my life. Thank you, thank you, thank you!"

11: Coughing in the Bushes

Our policy in Vice was to respond to citizen complaints. Some of the complaints were from women who lived in areas where prostitutes worked and displayed their attributes. Some of these women were solicited by "johns" who had mistaken them for actual streetwalkers. Some of the complaints were by men who saw men having some form of sex with other men in public restrooms.

One complaint we received was from neighbors living near the meandering road that went from Ocean Boulevard to the parking lot at Cherry Beach. The complaint was that from dusk until dawn they would see men going into the huge oleander bushes that bordered the road. They would hear grunts, moans, and profane language from their patios.

One night, Bobby and I decided to check out the bushes by that road. Just before sunset, we went into the bushes. There were, indeed, trails in the bushes. There were also large clumps of Vaseline stuck between branches of the oleander bushes. We also found some Vaseline jars in a couple places. Bobby and I found a suitable place to sit down. We waited a few minutes for the sun to sink below the horizon. We were planning to wait until we heard some activity in the bushes, locate the action, turn on our flashlights, and make arrests if violations were occurring. We didn't have to wait long.

We heard what sounded like two individuals making their way into the bushes, a little uphill and behind us. We figured we would wait a couple of minutes to give the men a chance to become engaged before we would make our move. Unfortunately, at this time, I had been suffering from bronchitis for about a week. I started a deep, throaty coughing jag that lasted about two minutes. When I had finished, a voice behind us yelled, "Boy, it sounds like that guy sure got a hot load."

Without skipping a beat, my partner, Bobby, called back, "He sure did!"

12: The Inventor

At the time I was working Vice, my youngest sister Dana was working as a sales rep for a pharmaceutical company. One of the promotionals her company had run was a pen that had their product's name on the side. Dana gave me one of the pens and showed me that it had a telescoping tip, like the old car antennas. This pen could be used to point out items when conducting lectures.

There was a commercial on TV during that same time that showed an Australian barbequing, where he said, "Put another shrimp on the barbie." I had practiced this Australian accent and had it down pretty good. I had used it once or twice when I was the bait arresting streetwalkers.

One day when I was driving the bait car down PCH, I spotted a working girl. I pulled to the curb about five yards past her. She saw me and came running up to the open passenger window. She stuck her head in the window and asked, "Are you looking for a date?"

In my best Australian accent, I told her that I was indeed looking for a date and told her to hop in. After she got in and closed the door, I pulled away from the curb and mentioned what great weather we were having. With a quizzical expression on her face, she said, "You're not from around here, are you?"

The accent was working great and so I answered her expansively, "No, I'm from Australia, Queensland, actually. You know how Australia is shaped like a terrier's head? Queensland is up in one of the ears."

With a bored expression, she answered, "I don't know about any of that. I got a D in geography. What kind of work do you do?"

I told her, "I'm an inventor of sorts. As a matter of fact, I invented this pen." I pulled out the pen my sister had given me. "It writes like a regular pen." I demonstrated by writing on my hand. "But, if you're giving a lecture or want to make a point, you can." I then pulled out the tip of the pen which extended its length from about five inches to about eighteen inches.

My "date" then started shaking her head and said, "I meet the most interesting people doing this."

The next minute, she made the solicitation. I gave the signal to the back-up car and I pulled to the curb. The back-up officers came and opened her door, told her she was under arrest for prostitution, and put the handcuffs on her. We already had three other girls in custody in their car, so they asked me if I would drive her to the station.

While driving to the station, I decided to maintain my Australian cover. I said to her in my Aussie accent, “I’m sorry, darling, I lied to you. I’m not really from Australia. I’m actually a foreign exchange police officer from New Zealand, but I fooled you didn’t I?”

Her response was emphatic, if not too original, “Yeah, thanks a lot, you fucking asshole.”

Section 2: Pranks

1: A New Coffee Maker

Occasionally, on the police department, as in life, funny things happen that are not the result of a prank or joke, but the result of just plain bad luck, fate, or Murphy's Law.

My first six months in Vice, I was the Administrative Sergeant. This was primarily a desk job. I had a civilian assistant, Fred, who was a Police Service Assistant (PSA). We would investigate and recommend acceptance or denial for locations requesting alcoholic beverage permits. We also periodically inspected the locations that had permits to play bingo and investigated complaints about any bingo parlors.

No matter how early I arrived in the Vice office, Fred was always there before me and had a pot of coffee ready. The coffee maker in the office made very hot coffee. I never drank coffee before I joined the Department. I really hadn't started drinking coffee until I left Juvenile and had to spend eight months on Graveyard Patrol. Graveyard was not my first choice, as I preferred Watch III, the afternoon shift. At that stage of my career, though, I was ready to leave Juvenile and go back to patrol. But during those eight months on Graveyard is when I really started drinking coffee. Even on Graveyard, the amount of coffee I drank was nothing compared to what I drank when I was the Admin Sergeant in Vice. I was drinking six or seven large cups a day.

One day when I came in, Fred told me the coffee maker was hissing and steaming, but no coffee was coming out. Fred said that was the bad news. The good news was Bunn had a distributor center in a bordering city, and our Homicide unit had bought a new coffee maker there and had received a huge discount. We got the okay from the lieutenant and bought a new Bunn.

That night, Fred asked me if he could take the broken coffee maker home and see if he could find out what went wrong with it. When I came in the next morning, Fred handed me a fresh cup of hot coffee. I told him that it tasted pretty good. Fred said, "That's the good news. I took the old coffee maker apart last night and found out why it wasn't working. That's the bad news. It was clogged with dead cockroaches!" I had been drinking six or seven large cups of coffee every day for five months and now I found out that the coffee had been filtered through dead cockroach bodies. I wasn't worried, though. That old coffee maker's coffee was always so hot that I was sure the heat had killed any of the germs the bugs carried.

2: Key Lime Pie at Johnny Reb's

After a long morning of arresting street prostitutes or lewd conduct suspects in public places, the day Vice guys occasionally liked to lunch at Johnny Reb's restaurant on Long Beach Blvd. As the name implies, Johnny Reb's offered Southern cuisine and hospitality. The walls of the restaurant were covered with old pictures of country scenes and photographs of sports figures from the past.

Occasionally, their featured dessert would be key lime pie. Jim, in particular, was fond of key lime pie. After a hardy lunch, Jim ordered the pie and was drooling as the waitress brought him his large piece of key lime. Before he could sink his fork into the enticing sweetness, Pat pointed to a photo directly behind Jim's right shoulder and asked, "Is that Ty Cobb in that picture?" As Jim turned to examine the photograph in question, Pat's fork snaked out and took about half of Jim's pie.

Jim examined the image and replied, "No, I think that's Lou Gehrig."

As Jim was turning back, Ted pointed at the picture over Jim's left shoulder and said, "No, Jim, I think that's Lou Gehrig."

Jim then turned to look his left and saw a picture that was obviously of Babe Ruth. As he was examining the photo, Ted reached his fork out and took the other half of Jim's pie. As Jim turned back to dazzle us with his knowledge of former baseball greats, he noticed that his key lime pie had vanished. The other four of us at the table looked on straight-faced as Jim ordered another piece of pie.

3: Cockroach

For a time while I was working Vice, the Deputy Chief of Detectives wasn't very popular with any of the troops. He was an arrogant martinet who thought he was smarter than anyone else and always spoke to subordinates in a condescending manner. He was always sending project assignments and reports back with his red pen corrections. Often, his corrections made sense only to him and corrected errors that only he saw.

One of the secretaries of a specialized detective unit got fed up with this Deputy Chief's antics. When she typed up a report that she knew he would see and "correct," she made two extra copies. She turned in the first copy, and when it came back with his red edit marks, she would turn in the second copy which was exactly the same as the first. When this copy came back with a lot fewer corrections, she turned in the original report, which was exactly the same as the first two, and the Deputy Chief would accept it! The secretaries and stenos all knew this was happening and had a great laugh at his expense.

One Thursday, the Deputy Chief of Detectives was out of the office. The Commander of the Special Investigations Division (Vice and Narcotics) held a staff meeting with all the sergeants and the two lieutenants in the division. He held it in the Deputy Chief's office. After the meeting, I went back to the Vice squad room. Jim was the only Vice cop present and I knew that something was up. Jim was pretending that he was doing something, but was looking out of the corner of his eye at me. On my desk was a large McDonald's drink cup, with a Post-it note on the lid. The note read: "For Sgt. Buz." I picked up the cup and, from the weight, it was apparent that there was no soda in it. I lifted the lid and saw the largest cockroach I had ever seen. It had to be at least four and a half inches in length. I slammed the lid back on the cup. Jim was giggling to himself.

I looked at Jim and said, "Come with me, Jim. We're going to the Deputy Chief's office." Jim asked why and I told him he was going to stand in the Chief's doorway as a lookout while I released our Frankenroach. We walked into the Chief's secretary's room and I asked her if I had left my notebook in the Chief's office when we had the earlier staff meeting. I was holding the McDonald's cup so it looked like I had just brought my soda with me. The secretary told me she didn't know and to go ahead and look.

As Jim stood in the doorway between the Chief's office and his secretary's, I went right over to the Chief's desk, pulled open his top drawer, lifted the lid on the cup and threw in the cockroach. I closed the drawer and we walked out. I told his secretary that I must have left my notebook some other place, and Jim and I went back to the Vice squad room.

When we came in the next morning, Friday, we saw that the Deputy Chief was back in his office. We went out in the field, made some arrests, wrote our reports, and went to lunch. After lunch, Jim and I rode the elevator to the third floor Detective Division. The Deputy Chief of Detective's secretary was standing in the lobby area. As we stepped off the elevator, she said, "All detectives have the afternoon off. We're spraying for bugs."

As we turned to get back on the elevator, I turned to Jim and whispered, "Don't say a freaking word. We're going to the movies."

4: Lights Out in The Men's Room

We were always getting complaints about lewd conduct violations in Recreation Park. Some of the complaints were about men going in the bushes around the outside of Blair Field. We dubbed the trail in these bushes "The Burma Trail." There was so much activity there for a while, the Burma Trail morphed into the Sperma Trail. Ultimately, the city cut down all of the bushes around Blair Field.

After that, most of the complaints centered around the restroom near the intersection of Park Avenue and 7th Street. As I recall, there were four doorless toilet stalls against an interior wall and a long trough urinal, opposite the toilets against the exterior wall. Above the urinal there was a ledge about two feet wide, about five and a half feet up from the floor.

Late one afternoon, about thirty minutes before sunset, Bobby, Rob, and I pulled up and parked the undercover car on Park Ave. First Rob got out of the car and walked into the park. A few minutes later, we saw him go into the men's room. A little while later, Bobby got out of the car and went into the men's room. By this time, the shadows were lengthening and dusk was quickly descending. I hadn't seen anyone enter the public restroom since we had arrived at the park, so I surmised that there might have been a sex party going on when Rob first walked in. I left the car and walked into the men's room expecting to see an orgy of lewd acts, while Bobby and Rob were making mental notes of who was doing what to whom.

I took a step into the men's room and let my eyes adjust to the little light that was filtering in through the vent above the ledge. I didn't see anyone or any activity. I called out to Rob and Bobby and there was no response. Then I remembered we had received one or two complaints about men going to the women's room adjacent to the men's room. I walked to the other side of the building and yelled for my two guys, who I thought had somehow escaped my vigilant observation and slipped out undetected from the men's room and into the women's room. There was no response. I had left my penlight in the car. By now, it was totally dark inside. I called out to Rob and Bobby once more and again was met with silence.

I walked back to the men's room and received no answer to my calls. I figured that since I was already in the bathroom, I might as well avail myself of the urinal. I slowly approached it. When I felt my knees bump the edge, I unzipped and began to take a whiz. Less than halfway through emptying my bladder, I heard a duet of loud, raucous banshee screams that literally scared the piss out of me. That was followed by an avalanche of laughter coming from the ledge. Rob turned on his flashlight and there, standing on the ledge, were Rob and Bobby, having a good laugh at my expense.

5: How Much Dog Weigh?

Some of us Vice guys took a few days off every year and went up to the Eastern High Sierras on an annual fishing trip. On this particular trip, the group included Rich, Jim, Pat, Chris, and me. On the last night of the trip we would have "turf and surf" (steak and stuffed trout). Around the campfire every night we talked about police war stories, fish tales, politics, and any other topic that any of the cops wanted to discuss.

At one of our campfire chats, Rich brought up the topic of his dog, Oofdalaina, which was Swedish or Norwegian for prolific crapper or something like that. Anyway that was the way we thought of Rich's dog after he told us his story. Oofda was a purebred Weimaraner. Rich's wife and two kids were begging for a dog and Rich kept telling them "no."

Rich finally relented when the kids promised to feed, water, and pick up after the dog. Around the campfire, Rich complained that Oofda constantly crapped in the yard. Rich pointed it out to the kids, but they didn't pick it up immediately, so he would go out there and do it himself. Rich said that if it was up to him, he would get rid of Oofda, but his wife, Sue, wouldn't hear of it.

After the turf and surf night we still had a lot of fish, so Rich invited us and our wives to his house for a fish fry. While Rich and Sue were entertaining us, Pat's wife, Georgia, bent down and was petting Oofda. She looked over at Rich and asked, "Why would you want to get rid of this beautiful dog, Rich?" Pat was running his finger across his throat, trying to tell Georgia to shut up.

Rich, who was occupied preparing the fish, didn't quite hear Georgia and said, "What was that?" Georgia repeated her question, despite her husband's histrionics.

By this time, Sue had heard the question. She turned toward Rich, pointed her finger at him (you could almost see the daggers going from her finger to Rich's heart), and said, "He'll go before the dog goes."

This was the hot topic in the Vice squad room the following Monday. There was obviously a sore point between Sue and Rich regarding their dog. With cops in general, and Vice cops in particular, one cannot show any weakness. Once a weak point is found, it is exploited to the maximum. The victim is not only psychologically kicked while down, he is cremated by a flame thrower and his ashes scattered to the wind!

With love, peace, and comradeship in mind, we placed an ad in the Long Beach Press Telegram. It read: "Free to good home. Pure bred Weimaraner. AKC papers. Call after 5PM. Phone number (xxx) xxx-xxxx." We knew that Sue got home at about 5PM. We don't know how many calls Rich and Sue received, but we know they got a few, because we made them.

Long Beach has a large Cambodian population. One of their cultural idiosyncrasies is that part of their cuisine includes dogs. Rob called one night when the Vice squad was working late and Rich wasn't in the office. Sue picked up the phone, and Rob, using a Cambodian accent, asked, "You have dog to give away. How much dog weigh?"

Sue, without missing a beat, said, "Oh, we already gave the dog away, thank you," and hung up.

A few days later, Lieutenant Mike came into the Vice squad room when I was there alone. He sat down and asked me, "Did you put an ad in the Press Telegram about Rich's dog?"

I answered, "Yes, how did you know?"

The Lieutenant said, "Rich was complaining. He told me that he had played a lot of practical jokes, but they had never cost anyone any money." The Press Telegram had sent Rich the bill for the ad.

Twelve hundred dollars for pure bred Weimaraner dog. One hundred and fifty dollars for a fishing trip. Twelve dollars and fifty cents for a classified ad. Priceless!

6: Crossword Puzzles

When working day Vice, I tried to get to work early so I could scan the arrests the night Vice guys had made, grab a cup of coffee, and do the crossword puzzle from the newspaper. I would bring the San Pedro News Pilot from my home. It just so happened that the News Pilot had the same crossword puzzle that the Long Beach Press Telegram printed. As the Vice guys came dribbling in, if I was stumped on a word, I would read them the clue to see if any of them knew the correct answer.

Now these were very good cops. Most had at least AA degrees and five or six had bachelor's degrees. Their fields of interest, judging by the answers they gave, did not extend to subjects of history, geography, or non-profane vocabulary. (They excelled at profane vocabulary!) They seldom answered any of my questions correctly.

Rich, who was an academy classmate of mine, however, did take an interest in doing the crossword puzzles. He started bringing in the Press Telegram every day and we would do the puzzle together. Again, the other Vice guys were of little help.

After a few days, Rich pointed out that erasing a wrong answer on the newspaper would sometimes smear the squares and would occasionally tear the paper. He pointed out that if he Xeroxed the puzzle on copy paper, wrong answers were easier to erase, and the paper didn't tear. Rich gratuitously volunteered to copy the crossword every day, and he and I would work them at the start of each day. The Vice officers began to respond by giving obscene answers to any questions Rich or I asked. For example, if we asked for an eight letter word for an army noncommissioned officer, the obvious answer of which was "sergeant," one of the clowns would respond, "dick head." The others would laugh uproariously.

One day, shortly after Rich started copying the puzzles, the Vice guys were suddenly able to give correct answers to our questions. The ignoramuses, who in weeks prior couldn't come up with a three letter word for feline, had suddenly been transformed into Einsteins who knew that the nine letter word for the capital of Nepal was Kathmandu, and even had the correct spelling. To compound my naivete, one day I found one of the copies Rich had made. I noticed that the correct answers were listed for that day's puzzle, instead of the prior day's. I told Rich about the mistake that the Press Telegram had made and pointed out that the News Pilot had not made the same error.

The following week, Lieutenant Mike came into my office after the rest of the Vice guys took off to do a whore run. He sat down and asked if I'd been doing crossword puzzles in the morning when the guys were coming in. I told him I had. He then explained how Rich and the other officers had bamboozled me by passing out the prior day's crossword puzzle with the answers, and given me the copy without the answers for that day. That certainly made me lose a little of my self-assurance as an ace detective!

Part 9: Back to Patrol

1: Sibling Rivalry

In 1990, after leaving Vice and returning to Patrol as a sergeant on days (Watch II), my niece, Susan, and her brother Richard moved to Long Beach. They were both in their 20s. They had been born and raised in New Jersey. Susan asked me if she could go for a ride-along with me, and it was approved. While we were driving around in my black and white squad car, we stopped for a red light. A car pulled up next to us. In that car were Susan's brother (my nephew, Richard) and his roommate. Richard yelled at me, "Hey, Uncle Buz, I didn't know you were working Canines."

Susan leaned forward to look at her brother, gave him a dirty look and just said, "Hardy har, Rich. Hardy har."

I just switched my gaze between the two and laughed at their sibling rivalry.

2: Russian Defector

Occasionally, I would have to fill in as the Day Watch Commander or the Front Desk Sergeant. When the regular sergeant at the Front Desk went on vacation for three weeks, I took his place.

One day, the Department's Intelligence Analyst, John, and the Intelligence Section's Sergeant, Bob, stopped to talk with me at the front desk. John said, "I've got to tell you what Jim did yesterday." (Jim was the same Jim who had been in my Police Academy class and whom I had just recently worked with in the Vice Unit. After I had transferred to Patrol, Jim had transferred to Intelligence.) John told me that Jim and his partner, Bill, were following an organized crime suspect. This suspect finally went home to his house in Palos Verdes.

Jim and Bill were driving through the harbor area of San Pedro when Jim spotted a Soviet merchant ship at a dock. Jim talked Bill into attempting to go on the Russian ship. They parked their car in the parking lot next to a blue federal Customs car that two officials were getting into. Jim asked them if they thought it would be okay if he and Bill went on the ship. The Customs officers told them that since the ship had cleared Customs, they didn't have any problem with them boarding the ship. Bill and Jim walked up and asked the Russian sailors if there was anything they would like. The Russians responded that they wanted American cigarettes.

Jim and Bill drove to a nearby store and bought three or four cartons of cigarettes. The Russians welcomed them with open arms and gave them a tour of the whole ship. When they got back to the police station, Jim told the Intelligence Analyst, John, about going on the Russian Ship. John told them to hang on a minute. John then called the local FBI office and said, "I'm calling to let you know that you can cross two espionage suspects off your list." When he hung up, John told Jim and Bill that the FBI photographs everyone who goes on a Soviet ship. (This was 1988 or 1989, so the Cold War was still on.)

I asked John and Sergeant Bob if it was okay for me to screw with Jim and Bill over their Soviet ship caper, and they both thought it would be a grand idea. A little while later, Bill came strolling past the front desk. I stopped him and asked if he knew some Russian sailor named "Vassely." (At this particular time, I was reading a spy novel and one of the characters was a Russian named "Vassely.") Bill got a shocked look on his face and said, "I think he was the first mate on the Russian ship Jim and I were on. Why?"

I told Bill that I had received a call from this Vassely, who wanted to defect to the United States. He was in San Francisco and needed to talk to Jim or Bill. I told Bill that Vassely said he would call back, and when he did, I would transfer the call to Intelligence. Bill went upstairs. I didn't see Jim that day.

The next day Bill came in a little early and when he saw me he called me several rude and profane names. He told me that after speaking with me the day before, he went up to the Intell office. The Chief of Police was in the office talking with John, the analyst. When Bill saw the Chief, he told him, "Chief, we may have a Russian sailor who is trying to defect."

Bill said the Chief turned toward him and said, "Oh, really?"

When the Chief turned away, Bill saw John swipe his finger across his throat. Bill then added, "Of course, this could just be a false alarm." The Chief then told Bill to let him know if anything came of the Russian defection.

I asked Bill if Jim knew about this, and Bill said that Jim had had a holiday the day before. Bill then encouraged me to "get" Jim, like I had snookered him. I told Bill he could count on it. A few minutes after Bill left, Jim came in. I stopped him and asked him if he knew some Russian sailor named Vassely. Jim stopped in his tracks and gave me the same response Bill had given me the day before, "I think that was the name of the first mate on the Russian ship Bill and I were on the other day. Why?"

I then expanded on the story I had told Bill. I said I got a call at the Front Desk from this Vassely and that he wanted to talk to Jim or Bill. I told Vassely that Jim and Bill weren't in yet. He told me he was in San Francisco and wanted to defect. I told Jim that I put Vassely on hold and called the San Francisco office of the FBI. They wanted to know where Vassely was, so I put the FBI on hold, got back on the line with Vassely who told me he was at the intersection of Commercial and Division. I told the FBI this and that was all I knew. Jim rushed upstairs to the Intelligence office.

What happened next was classic Jim. He burst into the Intelligence office. John was the only one in the office at the time and he was talking on the phone. Jim said, "John, I think one of the Russian sailors from that ship is trying to defect."

John stopped his phone conversation for a second and said, "Don't do a thing until I get off the phone." When Jim gets an idea in his head, he is unstoppable. He fidgeted around for a few minutes and then picked up the phone and dialed the San Francisco FBI office. He told the agent that answered the phone that he was inquiring about the Russian sailor who was defecting in their city.

The agent told Jim that the Russian sailor wasn't in San Francisco, he was in Sacramento, and that he wasn't trying to defect, they were about to arrest him for espionage. The agent then transferred Jim to the Sacramento FBI office.

(Just by the grace of God, the FBI was tailing a Russian sailor they were about to arrest for spying.) While Jim was trying to explain to the Sacramento FBI agent that he wasn't interested in the spy sailor, he was looking for the defecting sailor, John finished his phone call and realized what Jim was doing. John yelled, "Jim, it's a hoax."

Jim put his hand over the phone's mouthpiece, looked at John exasperatedly, and said, "It's a hoax?" After John explained the practical joke to Jim, he called down to the front desk and vowed to get even with me, if it was the last thing he ever did.

3: Jim's Revenge

While I was working the Front Desk, Intelligence had transferred Terry in as a sergeant. Terry, Jim and I had worked together in Vice. One day, Terry and John stopped at the front desk to shoot the bull. Terry said that he had heard that I might transfer to another PD. He asked if I was trying for Pismo Beach PD or the Morro Bay PD. When I told him that it was Pismo Beach that I had applied for, Terry told me that Jim was telling everyone that I was trying to get on the Morro Bay Police Department. I told Terry and John to just let Jim keep thinking that.

About a week later, I received a letter at home. It was in an envelope with the Morro Bay Police Department logo on the return address corner and was postmarked in Morro Bay. I opened the letter and found that it was allegedly from their personnel director. The letter stated that my application for the sergeant's position had been accepted and that I was supposed to have a "pre-employment" interview on a Wednesday that was about a week away.

Now Wednesday was one of my regular work days, so I would have had to burn a holiday or some banked overtime in order to make that interview. Of course, I hadn't applied at Morro Bay PD, so I knew this was a prank. Since only one guy on the whole Long Beach Police Department thought I had applied at Morro Bay instead of Pismo Beach, I knew that Jim had enacted this elaborate hoax. I was also pretty sure Jim had spoken about having a buddy who was on Morro Bay PD, which would explain the Morro Bay PD stationery and postmark.

I immediately called Jim. When I told him that I had applied at the Pismo Beach Police Department and not Morro Bay PD, his voice broadcast the disappointment that his practical joke hadn't worked.

4: Ernie Gets Embarrassed

While working Day Patrol in between stints at the Front Desk, I got to hop in a black and white and work the streets. Normally, sergeants didn't receive calls for service, but we would roll to assist our units on calls and were required to respond to any call that required two or more units. One Sunday, radio traffic was slow and I decided to drive to the Belmont Pier area. I was driving near the pier and I noticed that the pedestrian traffic on the sidewalk was pretty heavy. This was not surprising since it was a beautiful, sunny Southern California day. I was driving slowly when I heard a voice, through my open driver's window, yell, "Hey, Sarge, how are you doing?" It was Ernie, a young, tall, good-looking police officer that I knew. Ernie had an extraordinarily beautiful woman on his arm. I had no doubt that he called to me so as to show her off.

Ernie had only been on the job for a couple of years and wasn't quite aware that it was indiscreet to put yourself in a position where another officer, either on duty or off, could cause you embarrassment, because most cops won't pass up such an opportunity. I saw my chance and seized it. I stopped my patrol car, smiled and said, "Ernie, how are you doing? How did your AIDS test come out?"

Had Ernie been more experienced, he might have answered, "The same as your girlfriend's, or boyfriend's, or wife's or sister's," or fill in the blank. As it was, Ernie had that deer in the headlights look and kept ping-ponging his stare between me and his beauty and sputtering, "Ah, ah, huh?" I just smiled, waved and drove off while Ernie figuratively flopped around like a beached whale!

5: Deputy Chief Gets Cut on the Nose

I was still occasionally called in to work the Front Desk when the sergeant normally assigned there called in sick or was on vacation. One day while working at the Front Desk, I saw Lieutenant Jim, one of the really good guys who worked Juvenile. He was about to get on the elevator.

Unfortunately, at that time, we had both a Chief of Police and an Assistant Chief who were not very popular with the troops, for a variety of reasons. One of the reasons was that the two Chiefs would open Internal Affair cases on officers, sergeants, lieutenants, or commanders who they thought were disloyal to them. Lieutenant Jim was sometimes a target of their ill will. Knowing this, I thought I would tell Lieutenant Jim a joke I had just heard.

The Chief was in the hospital with some gastrointestinal problem. I asked Lieutenant Jim if he was aware that the

Assistant Chief was also in the hospital. Lieutenant Jim kept saying, "What? What are you trying to say?"

I repeated my question several times, but not too loudly since it was considered disloyal to joke about the Chief or the Assistant Chief. Finally, I said a little bit louder, "Yeah, the Assistant Chief is in the hospital, too. He received a severe cut on his nose when they were operating on the Chief."

Lieutenant Jim, kept saying, "Speak up and stop mumbling, I can't hear you." Just then the Chief of Detectives walked past us. I wasn't sure, but I thought he might have heard my joke.

The next day, I was called into the Patrol Commander's office. With him was one of the Administrative Commanders. They closed the door and told me that I was not in trouble and that I was not facing discipline, so I would not need a Police Officers Association representative. They then asked me if I had told Lieutenant Jim a joke the day before. They also asked if he had laughed at the joke. I said that the lieutenant hadn't laughed because I couldn't get him to understand it. The Commanders asked me what I meant by that and I told them, "I kept trying to tell him the joke, but Lieutenant Jim couldn't hear it. He's getting a little old now. I think you should send him for a retention physical because he can't hear a normal conversation."

I really just figured that Jim had seen the Chief of Detectives approaching and was trying to get me to shut up until he passed by. The two Commanders had me tell them my joke and then write it out. (In a side note, a year or so after the Chief of Police and the Assistant Chief were forced to retire, the Labor Relations Lieutenant, Mike, came to my office. He showed me my handwritten joke with notes from the Commanders, and asked if I wanted it in my Personnel File. I told him that I did not want it there and Mike said, "I didn't think so." He wadded it up and threw it in the round file.)

Later that day, I saw Lieutenant Jim in the parking lot. I asked him if the two Commanders had questioned him about the joke and he told me that they had. He asked me what I had told them. I said that he, Lieutenant Jim, didn't hear the joke and, therefore, didn't laugh. I also told him that I had suggested to the two Commanders that Lieutenant Jim have his hearing tested for a retention physical because he couldn't hear.

Lieutenant Jim started guffawing and said, "I told them that the Department needed to send you to a speech therapist because you mumbled so badly you couldn't be understood."

Part 10: Detective Sergeant Once Again

After a couple of years in Patrol, I went back to the Detective Bureau, first as a Sergeant in Auto Theft, then as a Sergeant in Gang Detectives, and later the Gang Enforcement Section. Two years before I retired, I transferred to Juvenile as the Night Sergeant.

1: Déjà vu

Sometimes an incident happens that takes you back to an earlier police occurrence. When I was the Gang Detective Sergeant, such an event occurred that took me back to the time I worked Patrol. One of my detectives was a young cop named Jeff. One day we were in East Long Beach when a call went out about a disturbance at Millikan High School. Since we weren't too far from there, we drove by. Whatever problem had been at the high school, it was no longer a problem when we got there. As we drove past, Jeff told me that when he went to Millikan High, he had come in possession of a dirt bike. It didn't run, so one Saturday Jeff and his dad worked on it and got it running.

Jeff told his dad that he was going to take it for a ride around the neighborhood, but his dad told him to just ride it around the block. Jeff, of course, didn't listen to his father's sage advice and rode the bike over to Millikan High. He told me he was riding it on the grass in front of the school when he heard a big car coming up the street. Jeff said it was a black and white Long Beach Patrol car. He panicked and took off.

He drove over to the flood control because he knew that he could get through the small chain link fence opening, but the patrol car couldn't. Jeff said that after he got into the flood control, he crossed to the other side. I interrupted his story and asked, "And when you got to the other side, you stopped and flipped us the finger, right?"

With a shocked look on his face, Jeff said, "That was you?"

"It sure was," I responded, "and if Zeke and I had caught you that day, you probably wouldn't be able to walk without a cane!"

2: My Revenge on Jeff

God forgive me, but an opportunity presented itself to me to wreak revenge on Jeff for flipping me and my partner the finger years earlier. A new lieutenant had just transferred into Gangs. He had a reputation as a good guy with a sense of humor. Unfortunately, the sense of humor part of his rep wasn't quite accurate. The department was expecting some type of problem and the whole Gang Enforcement Section was being held in reserve in a large vacant lot. We were provided with a couple of port-a-potties on a trailer. We were just sitting in our cars for hours waiting for something to happen.

Jeff was in the car with me and was telling me about the prank war he was having with Rubio, one of the other Gang detectives. An idle mind really is the devil's workshop. After a couple of hours of sheer boredom, sitting in a car with Jeff, waiting to see if anything would happen that would require us to take some police action, I saw something that immediately relieved my tedium.

I saw our new lieutenant going into one of the port-a-potties. With exquisite timing, I smacked Jeff's shoulder and said, "Look, Rubio just went into the shitter," just as the door was closing. Jeff got a big smile on his face and said, "I'll get that rat bastard, now." Jeff jumped out of our car, ran over to the port-a-potty the lieutenant had just entered, and placed his pen in the hole in the two brackets that effectively locked the door from the outside.

A minute or so later, when the door started to rattle, Jeff's smile broadened and he started giggling audibly. The smile and giggling stopped instantly when the lieutenant's voice boomed out, "Real funny, let me out of here." As Jeff sheepishly removed the pen, the door slammed open and the lieutenant looked down on Jeff and said, "I'll remember this, Jeff." Later, Jeff told me it took a couple of months for him to get back on the lieutenant's good side.

3: Once Again Jeff Embarrasses Himself

A few months after that, the Deputy Chief of Detectives' secretary came around to all of the detectives' offices in mid-morning. She asked all of them to go to the Chief's office because it was his birthday and they were serving coffee, ice cream, and cake. I was busy doing a project assignment and didn't go. Jeff couldn't resist the ice cream and cake and walked down to the Chief's office. Ten minutes later, Jeff returned. He looked fidgety and nervous. I asked him what had happened to cause him such distress. "The Deputy Chief is going to kill me," he said.

After singing Happy Birthday to the Deputy Chief, his secretary and an elderly lady started handing out the cake and ice cream. Jeff said that he was about halfway through his ice cream and cake, when the elderly lady came up and asked him how the birthday cake was, Jeff told her it was excellent. Then he told her, "You must be very proud of your son," nodding toward the Deputy Chief. The woman scowled at his answer and said quite loudly, "That's not my son, he's my husband." The Deputy Chief turned and glared at Jeff as he dropped his half eaten cake and ice cream into the trash can and slunk out the door.

4: Dare to Say No

A good prankster lives to get revenge. The old adage that revenge is best served cold is true, for two reasons. First, if your revenge is delivered too quickly, it often lacks a thoroughly thought out plan. Second, if the revenge is presented too soon after you have been victimized, your victim will know for sure that you are responsible.

Prior to transferring to the Forgery/Fraud unit sergeant's position, Chris had been the D.A.R.E. Sergeant. As part of the school anti-drug program, the unit developed trading cards with all of the D.A.R.E. Officers pictured at various locations throughout Long Beach.

Chris's card had his picture in a park with the Queen Mary in the background. Like a lot of these cards, it had "*DARE*" scrolled in red, followed by "Dare to say no to drugs" along the bottom of the card.

Some months after discovering my "Junior Sergeant" business cards, I was in Chris's Forgery/Fraud office, and I noticed his D.A.R.E. card. As true believer, I saw this for what it was: Divine Intervention!

The gang unit had just obtained a piece of equipment that enabled us to make exact copies of photos and documents. A week or so later, When Chris took a day off, I went down to his office and took his DARE card off the bulletin board next to his desk. I used our equipment in Gangs and made an exact duplicate of Chris's card, except I changed the wording at the bottom. The new card identified Sergeant Chris as the D.A.R.E. Sergeant, followed by the phrase "Dare to be Gay." I then put this card back on Chris's bulletin board. Everyone in Forgery/Fraud saw me and knew that I had done this, but nobody said anything. It took Chris two months before he discovered it! I would probably be fired or given a long suspension for insensitivity in today's politically correct atmosphere, but back then we all enjoyed the "gotcha."

5: Another Card Trick

I wasn't the only victim of the Forgery/Fraud Dynamic Duo of Chris and Debby. Greg, a very good, hardworking, and dedicated detective also worked in that unit. The two co-conspirators also sabotaged Greg's business cards. Halfway down his box of cards, they put in a batch of business cards that looked closely like the real ones. Instead of having his real name, the bogus cards read, "Detective Egg McMuffin," a close approximation of his true name.

At a regional meeting of all of local law enforcement Forgery/Fraud investigators, Greg started passing out his business cards. When one of the detectives from one of the other departments asked Greg who Detective Egg McMuffin was, Greg discovered he had passed out several of the bogus cards. I don't know if he did, but I sincerely hope Greg repaid his sergeant and secretary for their treachery.

6: Proper Attire for the Occasion

Chris lived in San Pedro, not far from my house in Rancho Palos Verdes. We carpooled for a couple of years in the early 1990s, when Chris was the sergeant in Forgery/ Fraud and I was the sergeant in Gang Detectives. We had a couple of funny incidents during that time. Since Gangs was doing a lot of search and arrest warrants, our uniform was jeans and a T-shirt. (We would put on a raid jacket when serving the warrants.) Chris, however, was required to wear a coat and tie.

One day I was driving us home after work. As we passed through the toll booth at the Vincent Thomas Bridge, my 1979 Peugeot vapor locked. Chris, in his coat and tie, had to get out of my old car and push it to the side, while I steered wearing my T-shirt!

7: Chris Is Not Headstrong

The day of a major early morning earthquake, I went to pick up Chris, but he wasn't at his house. I thought I may have made a mistake and it was Chris's turn to drive. I went home and called, but there was no answer. I drove to work without him. He called an hour or so later and explained that he had awakened during the earthquake and forgot he was sleeping on the living room sofa. Chris jumped up, tripped over the coffee table, and struck his head on the corner of a cabinet, causing a laceration. His wife had to take him to the Emergency Room to get his noggin stitched up.

I found an old football helmet and, at the next detective staff meeting, had the lieutenant present it to Chris as the only Long Beach Police officer who was injured during the Sylmar Earthquake. I am nothing, if not compassionate!

8: Ride of the Valkyries

When Chris drove, he liked to listen to classical music. Driving home one night, "*Ride of the Valkyries*" came on the radio. Chris, rather pompously I thought, turned to me and said, "That's Ride of the Valkyries by Wagner." (Of course, Chris pronounced the great composer's name Vogner, thinking I would be intimidated by the German pronunciation.)

I responded, "No, it isn't."

Chris, a little more emphatically, argued, "Yes, it is."

More forcefully, I reiterated my first response, "No, it's not!"

In a vain attempt to impress me with his expertise on the subject, Chris said, "Buz, I took a classical music course at Cal State Long Beach."

"I don't care what course you took or where you took it, that is not Ride of the Valkyries by Wagner," I retorted, pronouncing the W in Wagner like it was a V, just as Chris had done. "In the first place, in America, we pronounce Wagner, Wag-ner, not Vogner."

Chris said, "It's German, that's the way they pronounce it in Germany."

"Well we're not in Germany now, so it's Wagner! The main point is that song is not 'Ride of the Valkyries' by Vogner."

Chris then, rather confrontationally, asked, "What is it, then?"

I tilted my head, looked down my nose at him and said, "It's 'Kill the Wabbit' by Elmer Fudd." I wish I had a camera so I could have taken a picture of the deflated look on Chris's face!

9: Innovative Police Work in Gang Enforcement

We started getting a lot of purse snatching reports from an area that was plagued by an east side gang. The gangbangers would ride up on a bike and grab the purse. Because they were able to pedal away so fast, the victims and witnesses were unable to make any identifications of the gangbangers we were sure were committing these crimes.

One of my detectives, Joe, worked this east side gang. Joe came to me and told me that he had an idea that would stop these purse thefts. Joe started writing tickets to every gangster he saw riding a bicycle. It was a violation for anyone under the age of 21 to ride a bike without wearing a helmet, yet no self-respecting gang member would be caught dead wearing one of those uncool bike helmets.

After a month or so, all of those tickets went to warrant for failure to appear in court on the tickets, and

Joe and his partner started arresting the gangbangers. As a result, the gang members stopped riding bikes, but they still continued to snatch purses. Gangbanger fashion at that time was to wear pants three or four sizes too big. This made it a lot easier for witnesses and victims to give accurate descriptions. It also made it easier for outraged citizens and police to catch the gangsters trying to get away.

10: Accidental Discharge in Juvenile

In the late 1990s the Juvenile Division moved to a former medical building on the 1900 block of Pacific Avenue. In 1999, I transferred from the Gang Enforcement Section to Juvenile as the night detective sergeant. My office looked down a long hallway past a small locker room, a very small gym, and a break room/kitchen. A copy machine was at the end of the hall next to the break room.

One day, I was doing some paperwork about 4:30 PM, when I heard a muffled "pop." It was Cary's last night at work before he retired, and he was at the end of the hall making copies. The day J-Car officers had just ended their shift and were changing out of their uniforms in the locker room. The popping noise had sounded as if someone had dropped a ream of paper. I arose from my desk to see if Cary was all right. As I looked down the hall, Cary looked at me and shrugged and I did the same. Ramon, one of the J-Car officers opened the locker room door and peeked out. I asked if everything was all right and he told me that there had just been an accidental discharge in the locker room.

I walked down to the locker room and, as I approached I could smell cordite, which corroborated the fact that a gun had been fired. As I walked in, I saw that three officers were in the locker room. Ramon was still standing at the door. Matt was standing in front of his locker holding his still smoking gun. Jerry was sitting on a bench holding his shaved head in his hands and shaking. I asked if anyone had been hit and they all replied "no." Matt said he'd just pulled his weapon out of the holster and it went off as he went to put it on the top shelf of his locker. There was a bullet hole in the wall next to his locker. The hole appeared to have a slightly upward trajectory. I went into the next room, which was the small gym, and saw that there was a bullet hole on the wall from the locker room, and one on the opposite wall into the kitchen. In the kitchen, there was a hole in the bulletin board on the wall next to the gym, and on the opposite wall above and next to the refrigerator. That was where the bullet holes ended. The trajectory was toward where Cary was making copies, but was in an upward path that would have been both wide and high from where he was standing.

I went back to the locker room and told the three officers that I had to make a report and would have to get statements from each of them. I knew all three to be good, hardworking, conscientious officers. I told Matt that he already knew he had to be more careful, but with his good record and no past discipline, he would most probably receive only a written reprimand. At this point, I noticed that Jerry was still seated, holding his head and shaking it. He looked up at me and said, "Sarge, when the shot went off, the shell that ejected hit me right in the head. I thought I'd been shot in the head!"

11: The POA Christmas Dinner Dance

My wife Judi and I went to a Long Beach Police Officers Association Christmas Dinner Dance near the end of my police career. I was on the Board of Directors at the time and we invited all members who wanted to attend. My academy classmate and ride share partner, Chris, and his wife Rita went with us. After a great meal, the band started and the four of us went out on the dance floor. The vegetable served at the dinner caused a gastric reaction in me.

While dancing with my wife, close to Chris and Rita, I felt a painful gas bubble form in my stomach. The live band was playing a long song. I thought of running from the dance floor, but we were right next to one of the speakers, so I figured I could pass the gas undetected. About halfway through this action, I caught a whiff of an awful, putrid, sulfuric odor. Chris's eyes started to cross and I knew he was smelling the same thing I was. I had to think quick to dodge blame.

I grabbed Judi's arm, turned to Chris and Rita, and said, "My God, Chris. Show a little class."

Rita looked accusingly at her husband and said, "Chris!"

Chris went immediately on the offensive and responded, "That wasn't me. That was Buz." It was too late. I had already poisoned the well, both literally and metaphorically.

As I was walking Judi back to the table, she said, "Chris blamed you. Was it you?"

I told her, "You know those Italians (Chris was half Italian), they can fart at will." When Chris and Rita returned to our table, Chris told everyone at our table that he and his wife would not dance anywhere near us the rest of the night. True to his word, whenever Judi and I danced anywhere near them, Chris would whirl his wife in the other direction.

Near the end of the evening, Judi and I were dancing to a slow song. Chris and Rita were about halfway across the room. Judi whispered in my ear, "Dance me over by them. I'm going to give Chris a taste of his own medicine." How I kept from blurting out a cacophonous belly laugh, I'll never know, but I was able to keep a straight face. As we neared our victim couple, Chris spotted us and danced his bride away, just as the song was ending. As Judi and I were walking back to our table, I was guffawing uncontrollably.

A light came on in Judi's eyes. Then a hate stare. "That wasn't Chris stinking up the dance floor. That was you, wasn't it?" All I could do was wipe the tears from my eyes and nod a yes!

Part 11: Other Stories After Retirement

1: Domestic Violence on the Public Street

After I retired, I was hired back to do backgrounds on new police and firefighter recruits. The technical term for this position was "non-career police officer," but everyone referred to us as "dinosaurs." One of the other LBPD retirees who also worked in Backgrounds was Mike. He related the next story to me, so illustrative of what pieces of feces the men are who mistreat women. Mike worked the graveyard shift, which started at 2230 hours, 10:30 PM to civilians. He lived out of town and, when the weather permitted, rode his motorcycle into Long Beach. One night, Mike was running a little early and so, rather than take the freeway all the way to the Police Station, Mike got off the 91 freeway on Long Beach Blvd and drove southbound toward downtown. While still in north Long Beach, a pickup truck sped past him. A couple of blocks ahead of him the truck screeched to a crawl and, as it rounded a corner, the passenger door flew open and a woman was pushed out to the pavement. The pickup then sped off down the side street.

Mike stopped to offer the woman some help. When he got off his bike, she started screaming, "Get away from me or he'll kill us both!" Mike showed her his police ID and told her to get on the back of his bike. He told her he would take her to the nearby 7-Eleven store and she could call someone to come get her. She reluctantly got on the bike and Mike drove to the 7-Eleven. He sat on his bike and waited while she made her call.

As often occurs in this type of situation, the girl's boyfriend (or husband) pulled up in his pickup. As he got out of his truck, he grabbed one of those small wooden souvenir bats they sell at baseball stadiums. He walked toward Mike, slapping the bat into his palm, and said, "You didn't see a fucking thing, did you?"

Mike pulled out his pistol, which if memory serves me well, was a .45 Long Colt revolver. Mike pointed it at the suspect and said, "Yes, I did."

At this point, this fine example of masculinity dropped the bat, began crying and sobbed, "You don't know the problems we've been having." He was still crying when the unit came to take him to jail.

2: "My Wife Told Me to Park the Car in the Back..."

While I was working Backgrounds as a dinosaur, my good friend, Jim, had the desk next to me. We had been acquaintances more than 30 years, both from Cal State Long Beach and in the Police Academy. One of the stories Jim told me was that, while he and Rich (another Academy classmate) were partners in North Long Beach, they were sent on a call to a senior living center, near where the Long Beach and San Diego Freeways intersect. This was a non-injury accident that happened in the rear parking lot of the center. When they got there, they saw that a speeding car had flown off the San Diego freeway and had landed on top of the only car that was parked in that part of the lot.

One of the center's employees told them that the owner of the car (that was on the bottom of the wreck) was on his way out. A short time later, an elderly gentleman came tottering out with his cane. Jim asked the man if that was his car on the bottom of the wreck. The old guy just stood there for minute shaking his head. Then he looked at Jim and said, "Yes. My wife told me to park it back here so we wouldn't get any door dings!"

3: The Coffee Cup

After I retired and was rehired as a dinosaur, I worked out of the Police Academy. There was a cadre of retired police officers who did these backgrounds. Four or five were retired from LAPD. They were all good guys. One of the LAPD guys was named Celmer. I don't recall his first name, if I ever heard it. Everyone just called him Celmer.

One day, after getting our assignments, I went into the break room to get a cup of coffee. Celmer was there and I noticed that he was holding a coffee cup that had the name "Williams" on it. This cup was rather ornate. It was circled at the lip and bottom in gold and had gold vertical pinstripes and a gold oval around the Williams name. I think it might have been in a gift pack for Williams shaving gear.

I pointed at Celmer's cup and asked, "Hey, why are you using my cup?"

Celmer answered, "It's not yours. It was Cecil's and he gave it to me when he retired."

I looked closely at the cup and said, "Cecil gave you my cup?" I then laughed and told Celmer that I was just kidding.

When Celmer went on vacation, I took his cup to the Ye Olde Mug Shop on Redondo. I asked the owner if he could make a copy of it, using a different name, and how much it would cost. He stated that he could make a copy for about five dollars if I ordered 100 of them. I choked back a grunt and said, "No, no. I just need one!" The proprietor said that with the gold etching he couldn't just make one, but he could make one in black lettering for nine dollars and fifty cents. So I told him to make it with the black letters and pin striping with Celmer's name.

When Celmer came back from vacation, I waited until I saw him get his "Williams" cup and go to get some coffee. I then pulled the "Celmer" cup out from my desk drawer where I had hidden it and went to the break room. I poured myself a cup of coffee, walked over to Celmer, and engaged him in conversation. In the middle of a sentence, Celmer stopped, looked at my "Celmer" cup, and said, "Where did you get that cup?"

I smiled and said, "Cecil gave it to me when he retired." We both laughed. I then told him where I got the cup and that it would have cost me five hundred dollars to have the Celmer cup made in gold. Celmer then suggested we trade cups. We did.

4: The Sweater

Tim and I both sat on the POA Board of Directors until Tim made lieutenant. Tim continued up the ranks to Deputy Chief. He then applied for and was given the job of Chief of Police for the city of Santa Monica. While he held that position, his old Patrol partner, Marc, retired. I went to Marc's retirement ceremony, and Tim and his wife, Lisa, and their two sons were there.

While waiting in line to get in, I noticed that Tim was in civilian clothes. He had on a sweater that was black in color with swirls of turquoise, pink, sea green, and coral. I asked him where he bought such a gaudy sweater, as I wanted to stay as far from such a store as possible! Tim told me that he now worked in Santa Monica, which was a haven for the latest fashions, and he didn't expect someone as "provincial" as me to appreciate such trendy styles.

During the retirement dinner, guests were asked to come to the microphone and relate any interesting or funny stories about Marc and his career. Tim went to the mic and told a few stories about working with Marc on patrol, and shooting together on our Department's Pistol Team.

I immediately followed Tim. I told the crowd that while I was on the POA Board with Marc, I didn't have the pleasure of working with him, like Tim did. I informed those gathered that, while Tim and Marc were working together in a patrol car, I was working the Vice Squad. One of my duties in Vice was to attend a transvestite fashion show. I then informed the assemblage, "That was the first time I saw the sweater that Tim is wearing tonight!"

Everyone broke into gales of laughter. Marc told me later that one of Tim's sons had just taken a big gulp of cola and had sprayed most of it back through his nose he was laughing so hard.

Days later, when I returned to my home in Prescott, there was an email for me from Tim, the soon-to-be former Chief of Police of Santa Monica. It stated, in so many words, that I was persona non grata in the city of Santa Monica and that my photo was plastered on every lamppost in that fine town. If my shadow darkened the pavement there I would be grabbed by one of the members of the Santa Monica Police Department and unceremoniously, and not too gently, thrown in the slammer for an unspecified amount of time. I am sure Tim was just joking but, just in case, I haven't been back to Santa Monica since!

5: Rap Song "F—k the Police"

For about the last twenty-five years or so, Bill, who was a disc jockey, played at all of the events for the Long Beach POA, which is a group that supports the officers and the Department. Bill is an Honorary for the LBPOA, which is a citizen who volunteers their time and money in support of law enforcement in the city. Honoraries are a great asset to police officers and the police departments they support. Bill is a great guy with a great sense of humor.

At one of the functions at the POA Park, Bill was supplying the music, as usual. During one of the songs Bill was playing, I casually walked up to him and asked if he took requests. Bill proudly proclaimed that he had over 5000 recordings, and asked me what I wanted him to play. I said, "Could you play 'F—k the Police' by Ice T?" Not being a rap aficionado, I was unaware that that screed was recorded by NWA, and not Ice T.

Flustered, Bill blushed and told me, "I can't play that here."

At another POA function, Bill fell for me asking if he took requests again. The third time I tried it, though, as I approached Bill and his equipment, he saw me coming and, before I could make my request, Bill blurted out, "No, I don't have that recording." That's not the end of this story.

After Judi and I moved to Prescott, Arizona, our friends, Dennis and Tina, visited us from Southern California. Dennis had worked with Judi at an electrical company. Tina worked for a dentist.

When I was telling them the story about Bill, Tina stopped me and asked what Bill's last name was. Tina told us that Bill's son was a patient at her dental office. Tina wrote down the information about the requested song and said she was going to "get" Bill the next time he brought his son in to see the dentist. Tina told all the girls in the office what she was going to do, and they all stayed within hearing distance when Bill and his son arrived.

After Bill's son was taken from the waiting room into the examination room, Tina asked Bill, "Bill you're a disc jockey, aren't you?" Bill told her that he was and asked her if she needed his services for a party or wedding. Tina told him that she was looking for a particular recording and thought Bill might have it or know where she could find it. Bill gladly told her that (by this time) he had over 7000 recordings and asked her what song she was looking for. Tina said, "Do you have F—ck the Police by Ice T?"

Bill looked at her quizzically for a moment, and then asked, "Where do you know Buz Williams from?" Bill immediately called me in Prescott and we all had a good laugh!

6: Joe at Schooner or Later

Judi and I went to Long Beach for a retirement party. The morning of the party, we went to Schooner or Later, a restaurant in the marina in East Long Beach. We were sitting on the inside patio area when I saw another retired Long Beach copper, Joe, come in by himself and sit at the counter. I knew that Joe may have only met my wife once or twice, years ago, and I knew he probably wouldn't remember her.

I asked Judi if she saw that guy at the counter. She told me that she did. I told her his name was Joe and that he had gone to Poly High School. Always a gamer, Judi went and tapped Joe on his left shoulder so that he would have to look away from me, whom he would recognize. When Joe looked at Judi, she asked, "Joe? Poly High, right?"

Joe smiled and answered, "Well, yes!"

Judi: "Do you remember me?"

Joe: "You sure look familiar. Give me a minute."

Judi put a disappointed look on her face and said, "Oh, Joe. I'm so disappointed. You were the first boy to ever make love to me."

Joe started sucking in air, pulled his head back and turned white. Judi thought he was going to have a heart attack, so she told him, "No, Joe. I'm just kidding. I'm Buz Williams' wife and he's sitting behind you at a table."

Joe finally let out his breath and said, "Thank God."

That's not the end of the story. That night at the retirement party, Judi was speaking with a group of women she knew from the Department and our Kop Out camping group. Suddenly, two arms wrapped around her and Joe stuck his head next to Judi's and announced in a loud voice, "Judi Williams, the first girl I ever made love to." Joe then turned and walked away.

Jeanne, who witnessed this scene, said, "Gee, Judi, I didn't even know you knew Joe."

7: The Hearing Impaired

Sometime after we moved to Prescott, Arizona, in 2004, I joined Lodge 19 of the Fraternal Order of Police. Most of the members who attend the monthly meetings are retired from agencies across the United States. One of our members, Jim, had retired as a ranking officer from Hawthorne Police Department in Southern California. I spoke with Jim often, as my Uncle Don Williams had retired as a sergeant from Hawthorne PD and Jim knew him very well. Jim passed away in 2017.

At the next meeting after Jim's funeral and reception, I was sitting between two retired Long Beach coppers, John T., a retired sergeant, and John M., a retired Homicide detective. Between the two of them, they had three hearing aids. This is what we, in police work, call a clue: a clue that communication between these two would be confusing at best. Several members of our Lodge, including myself, had gone to Jim's funeral and wake. One of those who attended was relating to the other members what a great and classy send-off Jim had been given.

At that point, John T. turned to John M., who was sitting on the other side of me, and asked, "How old was Jim?"

John M. looked at John T. and answered, "No, he was on Hawthorne PD."

Unable to control myself, I let out a loud guffaw which required me to explain what was said to the rest of the members who all began laughing. I'm sure Jim would have gotten a big kick out of this miscommunication too.

Epilogue

There are many articles, studies, and books, both fiction and nonfiction, regarding the darker side of the lives of those in law enforcement. These writings will accurately point out the higher than average divorce rate, suicide rate, and lower longevity after retirement. But cops, like every other profession, are individuals. There are officers who see everything in a negative light and have sour dispositions. Thankfully, most of those leave law enforcement or get off the streets early in their careers. After a 29-year career, I've seen them all: the happy, the chronic complainer, the positive, the hard charger, and the lazy. Those who are the best cops last a career and take the job seriously. Most of the time, they leave the bad, sad, and heartbreaking memories at the station before they go home. They will take home the funny things that happen on the street, the pranks and the jokes played on other cops, civilian employees, and citizens. They relish the retelling of these things to other officers and friends and family.

I once wrote an article for the Long Beach Police Officers Association's periodical, *The Rap Sheet,* about cops telling each other war stories. Law enforcement officers, regardless of rank, will relate stories about when they were on the bricks as an officer or a sergeant or, occasionally, a street lieutenant. Even in a group of command officers, you will rarely, if ever, hear a story about "what a great staff meeting we had back in May of '97" or how "I realigned the Record Bureau's computer system to be more efficient." That's because these stories are mundane and quite boring when compared to "the burglar I finally chased down after 10 blocks, over fences and backyards" or "the liquor store robber I shot my second day out of the Academy."

This should be a lesson to police administrators: your attitude, sense of humor, and remembering what it is like on the streets has a direct effect on the morale of the men and women you command. I have worked under great chiefs of police and some very crappy ones. Under one of the latter, I went to work every day just trying to do my job to the best of my ability, wondering what I might do that could get me fired or major days off without pay. I tried to keep in mind what my dad told me when I became a police officer: "Do your job in spite of who you work for, since often you won't do it BECAUSE of who you work for."

Good leadership engenders loyalty. I've worked for higher ranking officers that I gladly went the extra mile for, any and every time, whether they asked me to or not. Others that I've worked for, I did the best job I could, but I wouldn't spit on their faces if they were on fire. If it didn't make them look good they wouldn't back anyone who worked for them and sacrificed good, hardworking police officers, who did nothing wrong, when the press and/or the public perception was against their actions. It was easier (and less detrimental to their careers) to give up the officers to a public opinion lynching than to exonerate them and take the heat from the press and the vocal citizens.

A well developed sense of humor is a necessary ingredient in good leadership. One of our Chiefs was contacted by a nationally known donut company. They were opening a new donut shop across the street from one of our substations. One of the donut company's executives told our Chief they were going to do a local advertising campaign and asked if they could use several of our police cars in a video, surrounding the donut shop as it opened. This Chief denied them the visual of our black and white Long Beach Police cars, telling them that law enforcement was trying to stop that "stereotype." Here's a clue to all Chiefs of Police and Sheriffs: we will NEVER shed that stereotype, so we might as well embrace it. It will show the people that police are not only human, we also have a sense of humor.

It is my firm hope that this book has done its part toward that end.

9781947521308